FROM AN AFRICAN VILLAGE TO GLASGOW

CALVIN NDLOVU

ISBN: **150283586X**
ISBN-13: **978-1502835864**

DEDICATION

I would like to thank Paul Gunnion of Greenhead Editorial and Publishing Services Ltd for helping with the editing of this book. I would also like to thank my beloved wife Sikhangezile (Skha) for her support and immense input. I am very grateful to Sihlangu Tshuma for designing the cover for this book. I would like to dedicate the book to my big Ndlovu family.

CONTENTS

FOREWORD

I was born in Nemane, one of the most remote villages of Zimbabwe. The village roads were very poor, education facilities below standard and health facilities non-existent. Growing up in such a village had its pros and cons with the disadvantages heavily outweighing the advantages.

With our village lagging behind in its amenities and infrastructure, on daily basis we had to grapple with the glaring realities of living in such an underdeveloped area.

This kind of environment is not conducive to a brighter and promising future and it could easily stifle the hunger and thirst for a better way of life. In my case, my home circumstances aggravated the situation as I was born in a very big and complex family.

I know, even today, there are a good number of rural children who still encounter the same problems I experienced. I hope relating my true-life story would bring to light their precarious plight. Secondly, I hope my story will motivate and stimulate their desire to persevere, regardless of growing up under such adverse conditions.

MY EARLY CHILDHOOD EXPERIENCES (5 TO 7 YEARS OLD)

"Mama, I've no relish for my isitshwala!"

"What do you expect me to do my son?" She asked. After a breather she continued, "Take 'bucket milk' or African brewed beer and use it as relish."

Our staple food is isitshwala, a very thick porridge made from pounded millet and is normally served with what we call relish. The relish list includes cooked vegetables, beans, milk, beef or chicken stew.

As we had no tap water at our home, we fetched our drinking water from a borehole or unprotected well and stored it in the kitchen in buckets. We did not have to boil this water before drinking it and this is the so-called milk my mother expected me to use as relish to make my isitshwala more palatable. Alternatively, she advised me to add the African brew. I do not know if she was aware beer would make me intoxicated, stifle my growth or worse still, make me dependant on it in the end.

What I certainly know now is that Mum was aware of her

financial constraints to provide us with a decent and proper relish. What she said was not new, as many times I finished a plateful of isitshwala using water or African brew.

We lived in Nemane, one of the most remote rural villages of Tsholotsho District, which is located in the western part of Zimbabwe. It is a drought-prone area where from season to season peasant farmers hardly harvest anything. Poor and primitive farming methods hampered the situation further.

During those days, men never used to work in urban areas but stayed in the village and solely relied on peasant farming and with no other reliable source of income, a drought year would be catastrophic to the food security of the family.

A few men trekked down the border to Johannesburg, in South Africa, to seek for employment where they could only get menial and low paying jobs like gardening, security or general gold mine work. The majority of them started new families there forgetting about their Nemane families who lived on meagre resources. The few who remembered never sent them anything, but visited only once a year and that was the only time some Nemane folks had a decent meal.

My Dad was a full-time peasant farmer whose sole reliance was the infertile Tsholotsho soils and very erratic weather pattern. With very limited monetary resources, our way of life was not cosy. Bread was a luxury and scarce commodity that we only ate during Christmas and we always looked forward to that period.

For recognition as 'man enough' by my community, one had to have many children, many cattle and goats. Even having many wives counted a lot. Since people used out-dated farming methods that needed more labour force, a large family gave that advantage. Hiring labour force was not the norm and worse still; most people could find the costs prohibitive.

For the above reasons, my family was big and very complex with my Dad having had three wives, my Mum being his first wife. The total number of children in this big family was twenty-three. My Mum had five children including me; the second and third wives had nine children each.

I remember the events fairly well from the age of five and by then, my two elder sisters, Sophie and Elizabeth were married and living with their husbands. Sophie was living in the city of Bulawayo and Elizabeth was married about a kilometre away from home. Effectively, my Mum was now responsible for three children Elias, Jabulani and I.

"Ungidlisa lamagalanyama," I cried drawing my Mum's attention.

That was my cry after every meal as the meals we had were not enough. From the age of seven, I usually shared a plate of meal with my two brothers Elias, fifteen and Jabulani, eleven. I always protested to my Mum for leaving me to share a meal with these two big boys. Because of their quick swallowing speed, I compared them with 'amaganyana' a word meaning wild dogs. As soon as we start eating, the meal would quickly vanish from the plate and as young as I was, I could not cope with their speed. Since I was too young, I could not even say the word 'amaganyana' properly.

My Mum told me, from a very young age, before a meal, I used to insist on a prayer and the following was my prayer.

"Njengokudla, Njengokudla, Amen."

This literally means, like food, like food, amen. I do not know where I acquired that concept at that tender age, as my parents were not Christians, but believed strongly in ancestral spirits.

Now that I am older and able to read and write I have come to learn what could have been my inspiration. When I read the

Scriptures, I learn about God who is love and when we love him or drawn to His love, it is because he first loved us.

As a child, I never thought my Mum ever felt hungry and that she always relied on food as a source of life-giving energy. After she prepared a meal, Mum normally would give us all the food and if ever she ate, she would eat only very little food. Often, I would enquire why she did not eat and she would say she was fine. Looking back now, I am sure she realised that if she partook of the meal, very little would be left for us.

I honestly do not know how she managed to maintain her nutritional status and for that, I found her to be a loving woman, full of compassion and empathy and always willing to put her children first.

MY CHILDHOOD EXPERIENCES CONTINUED

The three families prepared food and dined separately and like Mum, my Dad's two other wives found it hard to feed their households adequately. Their problems were even worse as they had more mouths to feed.

As the head of the entire family, my Dad was the most privileged person and always had adequate food since he received food from each of the three family units. He got the best and unlike the children, he never had 'bucket milk' or beer for his relish and that special treatment was reminiscent of the privileges rendered to most men of his days.

Our mothers and all the children knelt down as we served him his meals, as this was the tradition to show respect to the head of the family. After he had finished eating, Dad would give the leftovers to the young children.

Sugar was a very expensive commodity to buy and only a few privileged families could afford to have tea. My family was one of those unlucky families that could not afford it. My Dad liked tea and was the only person in the family who was entitled to it and the rest of the family only had tea during Christmas or when one of my sisters visited from the city.

"Mum, why does Dad have tea while we don't?" One of my half sisters, Margaret, asked her Mum.

"He doesn't have the money to buy for such a big family as you know sugar is expensive," her Mum reassured her affectionately.

"If it's expensive, how come he affords for himself?" Margaret probed more.

"Margie, you should respect! You should know who you are!" her mother reminded her.

"One day I'll be employed and have tea in abundance," Margaret aired her sentiments in a displeased mood.

My Mum and my Dad's other two wives took turns in making tea for him and despite doing so; it was very rare that they had a share, however it did not bother them much though as it was the village norm.

My Dad liked tea enriched with goat's milk and whenever milk was not enough, he would complain. One day when there was very little milk, my Dad demanded an explanation from my Mum.

"I don't know why Tennyson milked so little," Mum explained courteously.

"Where was the boy who normally does that?" Dad enquired angrily.

"He was still in bed."

"That's not a good reason to rob me of my good tea. Please next time you should make sure the right boy does the job."

I was my Dad's favourite son for milking goats and Dad preferred me because I always managed to bring more milk than the other boys did. To be frank, I was not always honest. If the goats did not produce enough, I would add some water to reach my Dad's mark. Ashamedly, I did that over years with no one ever discovering my deceit. Even though I used to do that 'noble job' for my Dad, he rarely offered me a cup of tea, but I had no hard feelings towards him as I knew and had accepted that tea was reserved for the adults. One day I would be a head of a family and would then be entitled to have as much tea as I wished.

We sometimes supplemented our diet when our parents were away from home by collecting wild vegetables, boil and eat them. Sometimes we would catch locusts, and roast them and at times, we would fetch wild fruits. While in the bush, we would coincidentally meet other children on a similar mission.

MY CHILDHOOD EXPERIENCES CONTINUED

Apart from our food needs, my Mum and my Dad's two other wives had the responsibility to buy us clothes and that was no easy task. I remember vividly that, for a while when I was about six, how humbly I used to dress. I wore 'ibhetshu'-a small piece of cloth, about the size of an open palm. Its function was to cover my 'boyhood', leaving the rest of the body exposed. Nevertheless, I was proud of my attire and saw nothing amiss about it.

I stopped wearing 'ibhetshu' when my sister Sophie bought me decent clothes from Bulawayo city and I felt proud and important in my new clothes. Some unlucky boys of my age continued to wear the traditional attire. I do not remember wearing shoes until I started school.

Since we had no beds, we spread our blankets on the floor. Our other problem was that we had inadequate bedding and as a result, I shared blankets with my elder brothers, Elias and Jabulani who were reasonable enough to allow me as a small brother to sleep between them. That was to make sure I was well covered and the close contact kept me warm.

On chilly winter nights, the blankets could not provide enough warmth and to counter that problem we made fire in our room to generate more heat. We kept the fire burning for most of the night and my two brothers were responsible for that. One time when asleep, our blankets caught fire, luckily Elias felt the heat just in time therefore averting a disaster. If we had lost our blankets in that fire, I do not know how soon Mum would have replaced them.

Our bedroom was a round hut with walls made of clay and a grass-thatched roof. The floors were made of clay mixed with cow dung to give it some colour and make it hard and smooth. Between the roof and the wall, they left gaps for ventilation purposes, but the gaps had their negative effect especially in winter allowing the cold breeze to blow into the hut uncontrolled.

Our home had several of those huts, my Mum had three, her bedroom, kitchen and our bedroom and my Dad's other two wives had three each as well. There was one communal hut used by all the girls.

The fire we made during the chilly nights had its bad effects on the thatched roof. It made the grass pitch black and brittle and, particularly on windy nights, fragments of smoked grass occasionally fell onto the floor. Sometimes, it accidentally fell onto our open eyes and it caused excruciating pain.

"Mummy, Mummy, help me!" I cried rushing to her for solace and pressing hard on my itchy eye, which had a foreign body.

"What's the problem, my son?" She asked pulling me closer to her.

"Something got into my eye!" I continued shouting.

"Sit down, I'll help you now," she said in a comforting manner.

"Please help me quickly! The pain is unbearable!"

The village had no medical facility, the nearest hospital was twenty-three kilometres (fourteen miles) away at Tsholotsho Business Centre, and to make matters worse, there was no telephone communication between the village and the hospital. On a day with no bus, a very slow ox-drawn cart would transport a person requiring hospitalisation, compounded by the sandy and bumpy roads; the journey took well over six hours.

Because of lack of health services, the villagers had devised traditional methods to cure some ailments and in my case, my Mum rolled her tongue around the affected eye to remove the particle. The results were soothing enough; it was as if she had applied some kind of balm. I experienced that misfortune on two or three occasions and I learnt to close my eyes as soon as I retired to bed. Even now, I still cannot get rid of the habit despite sleeping in a modern house. As soon as the bedroom lights are off, I quickly close my eyes regardless that I may still be wide-awake and chatting to my wife!

It was common in those bedrooms at night that we would relate to each other what transpired during the day. My elder brothers emphasised the importance of growing up as a 'hero' feared by other boys in the community, Jabulani, in particular, stressed that I should learn to defend myself.

The set up of our home was more or less a rectangular shape. The three huts used as kitchens formed the back row, followed by the three bedrooms for our mothers and then the three huts used by the boys from the respective family units. All the doors faced westwards where the main entrance of the home was while at the back there was a small gate. The home was fenced using dried logs dug onto the ground and we used the same type of logs to close the entrances. We only closed the gates at night or during the day, if everyone was away from home.

My Mum's huts, as the head wife, made the centre row and on

the left flank were the huts of the third wife and the right for the second. Standing adjacent to the bedroom of the second wife was a communal hut used by all the girls, the only hut out of the lines.

Our compound was just sandy with no single flower. A big indigenous tree within the home provided us with shade during a hot day.

At the front of the home were two kraals. The kraals built from dried logs of wood were for the goats and the other for cattle. They were very strong to stop the livestock from breaking loose and wandering into the fields. About fifty metres from the kraals was another big tree, which my Dad used as a workshop for his carpentry. After this, there was a well-knit bush, which we used for our toilet needs since we had no toilets. One would have expected the bush to be always messy, but surprisingly, that was not the case. The many black beetles, which needed the raw material, helped to clear the place.

At the back of our home was a very big open space, about the size of two football pitches and it also extended to the left and right flanks of the home. The space had sandy soils resembling a mini desert, very clean and clear of any thorns or vegetation. I learnt that it was a disused garden, abandoned years back when the soils became unproductive. Around that old field was thick vegetation.

The deserted field was our favourite spot – an ideal playground, which we used at night. On a full moon with a clear sky and cool evening, the place looked wonderful and enticing. It was the place where the children from neighbourhood joined us to come and perfect our sporting skills.

Our village was sparsely populated and as a result, homes were a distance from each other. In between the homes were bushes which obscured the visibility of other homes within the locality.

I do not recall receiving clothes from my Dad or seeing him buy for any member of the family. Even if he felt so inclined, it would have been mammoth task to clothe twenty-three children! Mum bought us clothes from the sale of our meagre farm produce. Occasionally she brewed beer to raise cash and the proceeds bought clothes, blankets and sometimes food. The other wives did the same.

My Dad was a disciplinarian, no nonsense type and firm and did not always need to use physically or corporal punishment as his authoritative voice and look was enough to keep us well behaved. He never entertained a child who physically abused another, as he believed the parents were the only ones with the mandate to mete out punishment. That policy prevented sibling rivalry and managed to keep the family intact and happy.

Mum was different from Dad in that respect as she was soft-spoken and to administer punishment was not her way. Whenever I did something wrong she only threatened me verbally without even a harsh look. Her threats never materialised and I do not remember her spanking me even once. Maybe I was not such a naughty boy! She was peaceful and never believed in violence and often said to me, "Son, if anybody wants to fight you, never fight back." She added "Kwabo kagwala akula sililo". All she meant was that if I avoided skirmishes, I was not going to bring disgrace or sorrow to the family and myself. Even today, I still try to live by her words.

Some evenings the entire family would come together and sit around the comfort of a fire listening to the experiences of our parents. It was also an opportunity for our parents to relate moving fairy tales. I used to love and enjoy those moments as they helped to reduce the stress of our village life. One of my favourite characters was Umvundla, the hare, who always played tricks on other animals.

My Dad owned a concertina, a cherished musical instrument he acquired during his working days in South Africa and he was so talented in playing it. When in high spirits, he would skilfully play the instrument producing some perfect melodious sounds. The effects of the music were electrifying and as a result, all the children danced to the tunes and it would be a perfect impromptu party just for the family.

❖ 4 ❖
I BECOME A HERD BOY (8 YEARS OLD)

According to my culture, it is a blessing to be the last-born child, the advantage being that you get all the pampering and attention from your parents and older siblings. This includes special food and favours. However, although I was the last born, I never enjoyed that privilege.

When I was about seven, two little children, Forester, who was five and Never, three joined my Mum's family. They were the sons of Sophie whose marriage had collapsed and she had brought them to my Mum, as she could no longer manage to look after them single-handed. That worsened our family woes as Mum had more children to feed and divided attention, the new arrivals and me.

At the tender age of eight, before I even started primary one, I became very keen to know what happens when older boys went to herd cattle. I therefore requested my Dad to allow me just for one day to join the older boys and he did not object.

We spent the entire day guiding the cattle to their pastoral area, following each move they made. To be honest, it was a very tiring experience and I never wanted to set my foot there again. When I arrived back home, Dad approached me for a feedback.

"Did you enjoy your adventure?" He asked.

"Not really," I replied. "It was exhausting and I wouldn't like to go there again".

"Since you survived you'll now join them permanently," he commanded.

That came as a bombshell, knowing my Dad meant what he said and I could not blame anyone but myself. That was the beginning of a long and gruelling struggle, a journey that was to last me for years to come. I would do that job until I was old enough to find a better job in town and if not I would remain as herd boy until I start my own family.

Every morning we left around 10am and spent the whole day in the grasslands. We followed the cattle everywhere they moved and our task was to make sure they never went astray. If they did and entered a neighbour's field, we would be in hot soup with our Dad and owners.

The bush was a rendezvous for boys and girls from all the surrounding villages. The boys were the majority as the girls were only from families with no boys.

During a good rain season, the dams and ponds would be full of water. Initially, the water would be muddy and after a few days, the water became clean and clear tempting us to swim. Those temporary water sources were free from the human predators like crocodile, giving us the liberty to swim without fear.

It was in those water sources that we acquired our swimming skills. Though basic, the skills helped us to avoid drowning. We were swimming stark naked as we never knew about swimming costumes. There were boys and girls, some 14 or even older, but we never felt embarrassed.

My early days of looking after cattle were really a nightmare. Imagine having a meal around ten and the next one to be around six in the evening when we got back home. Our parents could not afford to supply us with provision to eat at the bush. Sometimes, our evening meal was not always sufficient to replace the calories lost running after the livestock.

As the days went by, I became used to my newly adopted life, my nightmare gradually turned into a normal life. I acquired the new skills necessary to survive the harsh savannah life. Hunger was no longer an issue as we conquered it by munching wild fruits and juicy tuberous plants usually bountiful during a good rainy season. The choice of wild fruits was unlimited. My favourite fruit became 'umthuduluka', a succulent fruit, like a wild plum and rich in vitamins.

If we needed to drink milk, we would grab one of the feeding goats and milk it. Milk was readily available because when we took the goats to the pasture we left their kids behind and would only feed when we returned in the evening. With no adults around, we were in charge of life in the bush.

We learnt donkey riding. Although my Dad did not own a single donkey, I was still able to learn to ride one as herd boys believed in sharing resources. Those without goats benefited from their friends. Equipped with those skills, we started donkey racing and that was real fun and a joy.

"Hey, come here. Fight this boy!" Jabulani ordered me as we met a group of boys.

"Why? He never offended me," I shook my head in disbelief.

"I'm the boss! You do what I tell you!"

These were some of the up and downs we encountered, older

boys creating needless animosity, forcing us to box, and wrestle and my brother, Jabulani, was one of the culprits. I fought several battles but never lost any, the only fight I nearly lost ended in a draw.

After the fights, they would force us to make a truce and never report the incidents to our parents. If one sustained an injury, we simply told our parents it was an accident as telling the truth would bring repercussions. To be honest, I never enjoyed seeing someone in anguish because of my actions.

As dusk drew near, we gathered all our livestock and prepared for our way back home. It was exciting for we knew it would not be long before we had our dinner.

"Boy, you should be wary when you go past this place. Mind Sibanda as he can pounce on you," Sfa, my half-brother warned me.

"I'm in constant check."

"When I grow up, I would I revenge on that obsessed man," Sfa declared.

"He deserves it," I complimented Sfa's thought.

Sibanda was our distant neighbour. Every time our livestock went near his fields, let alone upon his fields, Sibanda would pursue us to our homes to punish us. During those days, it was a community norm to enter your neighbour's home and punish his children if the cattle entered their fields.

We hated him so much because of his obsession for liking corporal punishment. Worse still, he often raided us at very odd times, early dawn as we enjoyed our sleep. In those days, pyjamas were unheard of and we slept naked. We did not even have underpants, as our parents could not afford them. Sibanda knew the whip would agonisingly bruise our naked bodies.

One would never go near him after encountering his wrath. I had seen him whip my older brothers and so the sight of him terrified me too. The route to the pastoral area passed near that scary man's home and every time we passed, we would be wary of an ambush.

One day at dawn, that sadistic man came to our home to strike. I am sure on his way he was full of rage mixed with joy, as he seemed to love punishing herd boys.

"My maize crop, my only livelihood has been completely destroyed. Those boys will learn the harder way. I'll whip their naked bodies," he probably murmured those words as he headed to our place.

When he arrived, he violently kicked the door open. As it was still dark, he could not see who was in the hut.

"I'll beat up all of you!" He shouted. "Today your bedroom will be your toilet!" he raged again with a frightening voice.

There was complete silence in the room and for a while you could even hear a pin drop, everyone appeared to have stopped breathing. Nobody moved an inch. I could feel my bowel opening and my bladder sphincter giving up. I had never seen that man so annoyed and I was afraid he would crush us.

Still mystified what would happen next, Jabulani suddenly jumped out of the blankets and headed straight for the door. I thought he wanted to bolt out of the hut and save himself from the man's rage. What followed was therefore unexpected.

"Maye babo… Maye babo!" The old man cried like a wounded dog. "Please let me go! Please let me go!" He pleaded for mercy.

My brother had grabbed the man by his 'manhood' and started to squeeze it. Despite the man's agonising plea, he continued to squeeze. He did this until the disgraced man fell to the ground. At that time, my parents were up and had come to investigate what was happening. It was then that Jabulani let go and ran away.

"What's wrong, Sibanda? Why are you yelling like a child?" My Dad asked.

After getting no response, Dad came closer to Sibanda and started shaking him.

"Sibanda, talk, are you alright?" he persuaded him.

"The boys, the boys…," he croaked, clearing his throat continuously. The words did not seem to come easily as the old man lay down holding tightly to his essentials and whimpering in pain.

It was obvious to my Dad the man had been hit by an agonizing low blow. Seeing his desperate plight my parents comforted him and apologised for the incident.

From that day, that humiliated man never set foot in our home. Every time we saw him, we would taunt him, as he was no longer that 'lion' that we dreaded to see.

Jabulani was proud of what he did. We were also happy for his courage because at least he had rescued us from that menacing old man. When we went to bed, it had never occurred to me why Jabulani slept with his clothes on. Little did we know he anticipated an ambush from ruthless Sibanda? He was in preparedness to take up the glove and thwart his move.

Nemane is a thorny place and we never had shoes because the vast majority of parents could not afford them. We used to walk barefooted and that never bothered or hindered us in carrying out our daily activities. We used to run even over thorny grasses as our feet had hardened so much that small thorns did not pierce the skin. Rarely, on very hot days, we would use tree bark to make temporary sandals, which would last for a day or two.

When we came home with some cattle missing, it was misery

to break the news to our Dad since he was so unpredictable and could punish you there and then. If, for example, he was having his dinner he would continue to interrogate you and unexpectedly, he would take whatever he was eating and throw it directly onto the offender's eye. He seemed to have been a good aimer, as he never missed. Those who experienced it say that the pain was unbearable.

I remember on one evening when Sfa, was reporting a missing ox and Dad was sitting around the fire with most of the family members.

"Baba, I'm sorry to let you know one ox went astray."

"What did you do about that?" Dad probed.

"I searched the surrounding fields just in case it strayed into them. I also asked the boys I met if they had seen the ox," Sfa tried to explain in a defensive manner.

"Was there any sign of the ox?" He asked further.

"No," Sfa nodded.

Without warning, Dad took a burning piece of wood and threw it at him. Sfa acted quickly, jumped and tried to escape. Miraculously, he did not sustain serious injury when the burning log caught his legs.

One day, someone discovered the remains of our goat buried on the ground. It comprised the skin, hooves and the head. The goat had been missing for about a week and my Dad had been aware of that. After searching for it to no avail, the assumption had been that a fox might have devoured it. The discovery of buried remains raised the suspicion that a human being had been responsible. My Dad thus instituted a thorough search and the investigation revealed that one of our cousins had slaughtered the goat and sold the carcass. Dad reported the matter to the police at Tsholotsho.

As one of the herd boys on that day, they summoned me to give evidence. My Dad accompanied me on that long journey to the court of law. Appearing as a witness could seem too much of a task for a young boy who had not even started school and could not read or write. Fortunately, the procedures did not worry me much since I did not even understand the court's proceedings.

I cannot remember what exactly transpired during the court session but what I can never forget is the delicious food I ate, beans and isitshwala made from refined maize meal. This was a major change from my usual millet one. Never had I eaten such tasty food before in my little village!

❖❖ 5 ❖❖
I BEGIN PRIMARY SCHOOL (9 YEARS OLD)

I began my first year primary school education at the age of nine. Some people might wonder why I started that late as in normal circumstances a boy of my age would have been in the fifth year or so. The reason was purely due to lack of funding. Twenty-three children were just too much for one man to support and as if that was not enough, that number continued to increase when some of my sisters added their children into our family.

School fees were compulsory and in our case, the family looked upon my Dad to settle the bill. With his limited resources, Dad could only afford to pay for ten children at a time. If one was due to start school, one had to wait until someone dropped out and as there were many children before me, I had to wait patiently for my slot.

Our mothers assisted Dad by buying our school uniforms, as he could not afford to settle both. As they were also financially outstretched, we had to make do with only one set of uniform. At times, we used old uniforms passed on from our older siblings, but some of these were either not in very good condition or oversize. School shoes were out of question because our mothers could not afford them. Luckily, they were not compulsory, as most parents could not afford them. I walked bare-footed to school, even in unfavourable weather conditions.

I did my own laundry from the onset since the fields usually kept my Mum very busy. If not in the fields, together with Dad and his other two wives, they would spend much of their time enjoying beer with some villagers.

Since bottles stores and bars were unheard of in our villages, neighbours took turns to brew traditional beer for sale. Villagers would then gather at the home to buy and drink the African brew. Mum was always well informed where beer would be and hence she earned the nickname 'Phembela'. She was given the name by my Dad's other wives. The name literally meant someone with a good sense of smell and could catch the smell of beer brewed miles away. My Mum was not even ashamed, but proud of her nickname.

They drank sometimes up to midnight and on their way back home; they would break into rapturous and unrehearsed songs. I am sure that was another way of temporarily relieving themselves from their disadvantaged way of live. Our mothers would sometimes stumble and fall in an intoxicated state but my Dad always appeared to remain sober. He even bragged that women were very weak that is why they got drunk that easily.

My parents did not leave us with prepared meals when they left for their beer errands. They left millet – one of our traditional food components. Although there was a grinding mill in the village, we could not afford the cost, my brothers had to pound the millet manually using mortar and pestle until it became powder. I also participated in this activity at a younger age.

Most of my older siblings were school dropouts and only a few completed their primary education. None of them reached secondary school and this seemed to be the trend in the village.

Most evenings the boys spent their time with my uncle, Dengenyeka, who lived with my aunt next to our home. Uncle Dengenyeka had worked in Johannesburg, South Africa, for many years. Moreover, during that time, he never visited home or contacted his relatives. He had never married and had no home of his own. He eventually came back after contracting a disease, which left him with a permanent physical disability. He had grown very old and due to those limitations, he could not do much to help himself.

Dengenyeka was a very good storyteller and most of his stories hinged on his experiences in South Africa. He liked making bonfires and this together with his story-telling skills drew the youth to him.

"Oh! This fire is warm" said uncle, enticing us to join with him.

"I'm also enjoying the warmth," echoed one of the local boys.

Such comments enticed us to join them.

"I remember those days, those good old days," murmured uncle nostalgically.

"When was that?" Elias, my brother enquired.

"When I was young and energetic and when no woman could not ignore my advances," uncle elaborated patting himself on his chest.

"Tell us more," Lawrence probed.

"It was when I lived in Johannesburg, the beautiful city of gold – the city where you couldn't see where the sun rises or sets. The sun was only visible around mid-day," he continued.

"Woo...I would love to hear more about that place" Elias

commented with great anxiety.

My uncle was also a good hunter and due to his physical disability, he used snares to trap birds and small animals like rabbits. With his catch, in some evenings uncle would make a barbecue, which he shared with us. We loved that and always looked forward to the next one. Sometimes instead of a barbecue, he stewed his catch and made a delicious meal and this made him to be popular with us.

When the tantalising aroma of the barbecue rose, my uncle would cut a piece and eat to determine if it was ready. This seemed to stimulate him to relate more stories.

He told us about the skyscrapers that were scattered all over Johannesburg and said they were even much higher than the highest tree in the village. Those tall buildings were the ones that obstructed the sun as it rose or set. The bricks used to construct the buildings were eye catching and the painted ones glittered as the sun's rays reflected on them.

Uncle took our imagination inside the buildings and we speculated how immaculate the place was. He talked of marble floors, the hanging ceilings and the beautiful chandeliers. His description was so captivating that we undoubtedly wished to seek employment in that city.

The shops were huge and the atmosphere inside cosy, with air conditioning to suit all weathers. He also told us of the items sold in those shops and the list was endless. The shopping mall consisted of a vast array of bars, restaurants, petrol stations, offices, libraries, and rented accommodation.

There was no darkness in that city, at sunset, the electrical lights planted all over the town provided light until the next day. Houses and streets used the same lighting system compared to dirty paraffin lamps and fire we used.

"Uncle, are you sure it never gets dark?" I asked with great interest.

"I'm positive! I think it would suit you well," he replied assuredly knowing I was afraid of darkness. The thought of continuous light sounded good to me. My Mum used to tease me that I would not be man enough because of my phobia.

The residents of that city were of different races, creed and nationalities because they came from all over the world and spoke different languages. He told us about many white people found there. Many of the boys had never seen whites before and they wondered what kind of people they were. I had only seen one in Tsholotsho, the magistrate who presided over my Dad's stolen goat.

He also told us about the accommodation which comprised of houses that were sparkling and comfortable. Those were mostly for the rich and they were marvellous – just plush mansions.

Unlike our village, which had only one common mode of transport, a bus, Johannesburg had countless cars, buses and trains. We could not imagine how a train looked like.

Uncle Dengenyeka told us about the many job opportunities that awaited us there which were very different from the farming and cattle herding ones we knew. The money earned from those jobs could make dreams come true.

"Uncle, we've heard of this land of opportunities. So, how do we get there?" Elias asked with great interest.

"It's simple," he replied.

It was easy in the sense that we did not need much cash to undertake the journey. Individuals used public transport up to the Zimbabwean/ South African boarder. They would then attempt to cross illegal to South Africa using undesignated crossing points on the Limpopo River. This perennial river runs along the

Zimbabwean and South African border and it is crocodile infested. Most boarder jumpers usually attempted crossing during winter as in summer the river was flooded.

Before undertaking the journey, my uncle stressed the importance of appeasing the ancestral spirits to clear the way of any obstacles. The ceremony involved brewing beer and the gathering of close relatives who would perform the rituals. They sprinkled beer for the ancestral spirits onto the ground, which was a belief they would be communicating with the spirits. The left over was reserved for the family consumption.

People crossed this deadly river in groups of about five and as they swam across, they carried sharp sticks to fend off crocodile attacks. If a member of the group was lost to the crocodiles, they attributed it to improper appeasing of ancestral spirits. Dengenyeka assured us it was very rare for souls to be lost to crocodiles or drowning.

After successful crossing into South Africa, the illegal immigrants continued the journey on foot, mainly under cover of darkness. They avoided arrest by the South African Police who tortured and then deported back to Zimbabwe. Those days, Nemane villagers did not know anything about passports or visas.

In populated areas like villages and farms, they slept during the day to avoid detection by the local people. Occasionally they disguised themselves and sneaked into shops to buy food. If they came upon a farm with edible crops, they would reap them without the authority of the owner. Since they walked, the journey took about three weeks or even longer if they went off track.

Uncle Dengenyeka related to us a story of a young man who was very desperate, as he had gone for days without food. Eventually, he came across a herd of goats grazing and what followed was one of the most bizarre incidents I had ever heard. He grabbed the goat and with his knife sliced off one of its hind legs. He then sped off, leaving the goat bleating and bleeding to its death. That day he had a barbecue in the bush.

If they were travelling through the game parks, they only walked during the day. By night, they made their beds in trees in fear of lions and hyenas that usual hunted for prey then.

"Uncle, that is scary, walking in a game park!" I exclaimed.

"It's not. Think of the prize – getting into Johannesburg," he reassured.

"I wouldn't sacrifice my life for that," I replied.

"Then you'll spend all your life in this dusty village looking after cattle," he said mockingly.

After the chilling experiences, many boys still wanted to pursue the journey to Johannesburg for greener pastures. Only a few like me were a bit sceptical, preferring to work in our less lucrative town, Bulawayo.

Some of those who managed to work in Johannesburg returned after a few years having changed their way of life. They talked differently and dressed in the latest fashion. Their families also benefited as they brought clothes and money for food. They also bought cattle and goats and as cattle owners, they started to earn respect from the community. Their success influenced some boys to track to Johannesburg; others had to drop out of primary school to undertake this journey.

❖ 6 ❖
MY FIRST PAIR OF SHOES (9 YEARS OLD)

"Look at my shoes! Are they not lovely? "I broke into an ecstatic song of joy.

"They look beautiful indeed, my son!" Mum echoed.
"I cannot believe they're mine?" I added.

That was my first pair of shoes. This was about six months after I started primary one and I found this too be too good to be true. It has remained as one of the most memorable days of my life.

The shoe was size three, black in colour and with a lovely pattern in front. It was my proper size as it fit me well. My legs felt heavy though the first time I had them on.

Before I started school, one local miller gave me a hen as a gift. That hen later had chicks and within a year, I had about ten fowls. My Mum sold some of those fowls and bought me shoes. I really owe some sincere gratitude to that miller.

I highly valued my pair that I kept them sparkling clean all times. Sometimes I would leave them home and walk to school barefooted to try to prolong their life span. I knew if worn out, it would not be easy to replace them. After school, the first thing I did was to immediately check on them.

One-day two boys who were our distant cousins passed by our home en route to South Africa to seek for employment. They had walked a long distance hence they stayed with us for a few days to regain their strength before resuming the long journey ahead. When I put on my shoes, one of those boys had this say.

"You've smart shoes."

"Thank you very much," I responded.

"Where did you buy them from?" The boy asked.

"They're from the City," I said as we concluded our conversation.

On day three, after the visitors' arrival, I went to school without my shoes. When I came back, as usual, I went to check on my shoes and I was dumbfounded when my only pair of shoes was not in its usual place. Straight away, I had a strong feeling I would never see them again. My heart started pounding, I became breathless and I then ran to alert my Mum.

"Mum! Mum! Where are my shoes?" I asked with my heart beating fast. Before she could answer, I asked her again. "Who took my shoes?"

"My son, I'm not aware that your shoes are missing."

"I can't find them," I said, my voice trembling. My Mum's revelation was another blow. Somehow I had a feeling my Mum could have seen them.

We then quickly went back into the hut to help each other do a thorough search and we could not locate them. The hunt continued outside the room but all were to no avail.

"What are you looking for?" One of my half-sisters asked. "I may assist you," she added.

"My shoes…. My shoes," I replied in a quivering voice.

"They are gone," she said.

"What?"

"I mean it!" My sister retorted.

"Gone where?" I quizzed her.

She then went on to relate what had transpired. Our visitors had resumed their journey and one of them wore my shoes. It was as if she had pierced my heart. Beads of sweat streamed down my face and in no time, I went into a fit of rage, throwing myself onto the dusty ground.

"Maye babo… Maye babo!" I burst into uncontrolled weeping.

"Oh, my shoes," I sobbed bitterly. Everyone there struggled to calm me down.

When I calmed down, my brother, Jabulani, decided to pursue the thieves. He followed them for more than ten kilometres (six miles) but never caught up with them. The news was the final nail on the coffin knowing it would be hard to find a replacement. Surely, it took me more than two years before my sister Sophie bought me another pair.

❦ 7 ❦
JOINING THE FAMILY LABOUR FORCE (9 YEARS OLD)

Despite the devastating loss of my shoes, I remained focused in my schoolwork. My family started utilising me to the maximum and it became no easy task to combine demanding home chores and schoolwork. It was more challenging especially during the ploughing season when Dad used to wake us up at 2am to go to the fields. The four to five hours I slept were inadequate.

We had no tractors to till the fields and therefore we used ox-drawn ploughs. Four oxen pulled each plough with two people in charge of each team. There were three teams working on each day. We named the oxen according to how they behaved, for example, 'Nice' was a very conforming ox. Other names included 'Stripes', and 'Black' given according to their appearances. Each ox responded very well to its name when beckoned as if it knew its name.

The entire family with the exception of my Dad and little children went to the fields. After we left for the fields, Dad retreated to bed.

The three families combined their work force when ploughing.

On a daily basis, we alternated working in the fields starting with my Dad's fields, followed by my Mum's and then the rest of my Dad's wives.

"Nice, stop! Where are you going?" I beckoned the ox when it went off track and if it did not comply, I whipped it. Shouting and commanding was the order of the day.

My partner's duty was to control the plough, furrow after furrow making sure they were straight; otherwise, he would get some blame for it. That job needed someone experienced and muscular as the oxen's force could throw the hands' grip off the plough. As I became more mature, Dad assigned me to the plough, which was a tiresome job.

The shouting and screaming was exhaustive and affected both animals and us particularly on a hot day. One day I witnessed a sad incidence when one of our oxen died while pulling the plough.

As we started ploughing very early, the moon provided us with light. If ploughing was on a school day, at sunrise we dismissed to go and prepare for school leaving the rest of the family working.

We did not have adequate time to prepare for school we just wiped ourselves and dashed. Fortunately, the school was only a stone's throw from my home. Most of the times, I left without having breakfast and if ever I had something, it would be cold food left from the evening.

As soon as my dad heard us preparing for school, he woke up, prepared his tea and after that made his way to the field. Upon arrival, he would saunter, inspecting the job done.

"Elias, this is not right. Your furrows are crooked," he would remark.

"We'll try our best, baba." Elias answered politely.

He would continue moving around the fields, sometimes uprooting any weeds he came across. After an hour or so, he would demarcate more area that he wanted the family to cover. He would then head back home where he would engage in carpentry or sewing. It was from the sale of these products that he raised the cash to pay our fees, but unfortunately, it was not enough to cater fully for twenty-three children and three wives.

We used to plough from Sunday to Friday leaving us with only one day, Saturday as the day of our rest. It was real hard work, which demanded lots of energy and commitment.

Although our Dad gave us too much work, we never grumbled but took the orders positively as we respected elders and looked up to them as our heroes. We understood our way of life and we knew that we had to sweat to get food. As the head of the family, it was his duty to instruct us. As boys, this inspired us, and we looked forward to growing up to enjoy the privileges of being a head of a family one day.

We normally retired from ploughing around 11 am and by that, time the sun would be scorching hot and we would be fatigued and hungry. We never had refreshments to take to the fields although occasionally we had our traditional drink, 'amahewu'. This is isitshwala mixed with water left to ferment until it turned sour ready to be drunk. The only setback about this drink is that it lacked proper nutrients necessary to replace burnt down calories.

Starting with the gruesome fieldwork before going to school was taxing and no wonder why our local school produced under achieving pupils. Schooling seemed to be for semi- literacy purposes as there were no role models in the community who prospered due to education

After school, we quickly dashed home because other tasks lay ahead of us. We were supposed to relieve our brothers from herding cattle. We had lunch on our toes and quickly rushed to the pastures.

We usually took over from Pedias who was very particular with time keeping. He always stressed that we should run when coming to relieve him. If he suspected any delay, he would punish us and intimidate us not to report to anyone. We suffered in silence and continued to bear his inauthentic punishment.

"Boys why are you so late? Were you running?" Pedias would enquire in a harsh voice.

"We were running all the way," I confirmed.

"When going home I'll check your footprints! If they show that you were not, I'll punish you severely tomorrow." He threatened.

It was a long journey and so it was virtually impossible for us to run all the way and we hatched ideas to cheat him. We walked with long strides, scooped a bit of sand to create an impression that we were running.

We took over and remained in the bush until sunset to start gathering cattle to head home. By then we were weary, undermining our ability to do our homework properly.

We had 40 head of cattle and a hundred goats, which our Dad bought many years ago when he used to work in South Africa. I gather he had started with just a handful of livestock and these gradually increased as years went by.

During those days, men enjoyed adoring their herds and they never believed in selling or slaughtering cattle or goats. Considering the number of our Dad's livestock, one would expect him to slaughter at least one goat a year for the hard working family. I do not remember him rewarding us. The only time when we had beef was when an ox succumbed to drought. The animal would be skinny and the beef of very poor quality.

We also tasted beef when an ox or cow dies of unknown

reasons. We would sell the excess beef of this carcase to our neighbours and they did the same if similar circumstances befell to them. I know now that eating that carcase was very unwise as this could have been a source for devastating diseases like anthrax or foot and mouth. Thank goodness, we never contracted any of those diseases.

Periodically, at Tsholotsho cattle pan, butchers used to come to buy livestock for slaughter. Parents obtained money that way which they used for buying food, clothing or paying school fees. Dad, like most of his fellow men, rarely sold theirs because of the belief in holding to their herds unless the beast was very old. That did not benefit them, as old cattle did not fetch much. Those primitive ideas were a severe set back to many families.

It is a fact that cattle benefited the family for ploughing, milk or pulling carts but they could also have been even more beneficial if our parents had not held onto them until they had less value on sale.

❖ 8 ❖
MY NEAR DEATH MISS (9 YEARS OLD)

Providing labour in the family came with its own risks as I nearly lost my life in one incident which involved my brother, Elias. As youngsters, we had no say but to conform. We respected older brothers as we did our Dad, taking their orders without hesitation. Our parents expected us to give our brothers that respect as a way of initiating older boys to manhood.

"You should lead the oxen while we go to fetch firewood!" Elias ordered. "We should be as fast as we can," he commanded.

"Yes, brother," I replied obediently.

Dusk was drawing close and my brother wanted us to go and come back before dark. It was a very chilly day and I had put on one of my father's old coats.

Elias jumped onto the ox drawn cart, started whipping the oxen so that they could run as fast as they could. I was running in front of the oxen guiding them with a rope tied around their necks.

"Nice... Black, Run!" Elias beckoned the oxen, whipping them in the process. This provoked the oxen to run even faster and my brother expected me to keep up with their speed. He seemed to enjoy the ride at my expense.

"Hey ... run, you sleepy head!" my brother shouted.

I held my oversize coat and tried to run as fast as I could.

"Run, boy! Run!" He commanded ignoring my efforts.

Eventually, it became impossible to cope with the speed of the animals. My heart began to beat fast and my legs seemed not to carry my body. I do not know where my brother expected me to get the energy to outrun the animals. He seemed to have had the impression that I could run miles and miles like an engine-propelled vehicle. It was not long before my brother proved himself wrong.

In a twinkle of an eye, one of the oxen, in a desperate process to try to avoid further whips, outpaced me, gored into my coat with its sharp horn, and lifted me up. During the pandemonium, the oxen and the cart came to a sudden halt. For a few seconds I did not remember what transpired. The ox then moved its horn and in the process dropped me on the ground. By a whisker through God's grace, it dropped me safely and my delicate skin was unscathed.

I breathed a big sigh of relief shivering like a reed in the river. Elias quickly jumped off the cart and came charging at me.

"Stupid boy, I told you to run and you dragged your feet. You'll learn it the hard way today!" My brother raged as he alighted from the cart.

Without empathising or checking if I had sustained an injury, he started whipping me with the same whip he used for the animals. I got the shock of my life and failed even to scream. If anything happened, I could have died in my silence while my brother took no notice of the deadly scenario that had occurred. After the punishment, he jumped onto the cart and continued with his orders beckoning the oxen and myself to run. What a stony heart!

We loaded the wood and quickly returned home. On arrival, I recapped what had transpired. I imagined myself with a gored wound-penetrating deep into my lungs or worse still into my heart resulting in heavy and uncontrolled blood loss. I also visualised myself groaning in pain and gasping for air. Chills went down my spine as I speculated trampled into mincemeat with all bones fractured by the animals and the cart. The situation could have left me permanently confined to a wheelchair. My imagination took me to my funeral and saw people standing next to my coffin paying their last respects and singing "No abiding city here".

Imagine, I was only nine and my brother was 17. What hard feelings, untouched by my near-death miss! That compelled me to report him to Dad.

"I nearly died," I sobbed as I reported to Dad.

Elias tried to intimidate me by winking and I did not pay attention to that.

"What happened?" My Dad asked as he tried to clear his throat. I told him everything and he gaped in disbelief. Elias was also close by and I anticipated what the consequence could be. My Dad bit his lower lip and steamed off with thunderous words.

"You want to kill my son!" He said pointing an accusing finger.

With no chance to run for cover, Elias stood frozen.

Still fuming with rage, Dad pounced on Elias with a thunderous slap on the cheek which left him dazed. I looked at Elias, feelings of sympathy gripped me, and I regretted reporting him.

Six months later, after school, I went to herd cattle as usual. I met my friends, as it was a hot day we decided cooling ourselves by swimming. We enjoyed ourselves forgetting the prime duty; herding cattle. As soon as we noticed, it was already getting dark. We gathered our cattle and amongst my herd, five beasts were missing.

I started to scamper in the bushes while my friends whistled, heading home. I was very desperate to recover the missing animals.

"Hey! What are you looking for?" I heard a voice from a thicket. It was Stewart, one of the local boys.

"The missing cattle," I replied hoping to get a consoling answer.

"They were found grazing in Mr Ndiweni's maize field," he explained.

Those were very saddening news and I could picture the havoc left at that field and I felt guilty of having a hand in impoverishing the Ndiweni family.

"So...what happened next?" I inquired with a worried voice.

"Mr Ndiweni has impounded them," he elaborated leaving my heart pierced.

I knew what was in store for me as I would be in trouble with my Dad, as well as Mr Ndiweni. Quickly from my memory, flashed the tantrum my Dad had when Sfa had a similar incident. I visualised the burning wood flying at me and felt butterflies churning in my stomach. I remembered that lump of food splashing onto my brother's eye when he lost some cattle too. I definitely knew that the same fate awaited me and this compelled me to devise a plan instead of simply surrendering myself to Dad.

As soon as I had driven the rest of cattle into the kraal, I vanished. I hid in the bush until I made sure everyone at home had retired to bed before I made the next move. I stalked home and sneaked into one of the compartments of an empty millet barn. Each chamber was half a metre wide, half a metre long, a metre high, and I squashed in because of the limited space. I was set to spend my night there, as I was afraid to join my brothers in our bedroom just in case they alert my Dad.

Inside the barn, it was pitch-dark though outside the full moon shone brightly and made everything visible. Since I was afraid, I could not sleep but kept peeping outside. Though scared, I knew the barn was my only safe haven.

In the middle of the night, I spotted a dreadful figure that left me shell-shocked. It was an old woman, stark naked and with chains of beads around her body and I could not recognise that woman. My intuition convinced me that she was a witch on a mission. As I was not sure if she was aware of my presence, I felt that the hideout was not safe any more. If she had seen me, she could come back and practised her witchcraft on me.

Full of fear, the only option was for me to vacate the site immediately. I made sure the spooky figure had moved out of sight and bolted out of barn like a bullet straight into our bedroom. Fortunately enough there was no locking system and in a flash I sandwiched myself between my brothers.

"Where have you been? Why are you panting?" Jabulani asked.

"Can't you hear what Jabulani is saying?" Elias echoed.

I was so petrified; I just pretended to be deaf. My persistent muteness put them off and they continued with their sleep.

The following morning I woke up very early put on my school uniform and quickly made my way to school before the rest of the family did. The thought of the punishment, which awaited me at home, made me absent-minded. One of the observant pupils asked why I looked unusually low and I lied that I had a nagging headache.

After school, I dragged myself back home. I had no other alternative since hunger was taking its toll and home was the only place I could get something to eat.

When I arrived, my brother told me Dad had sent a delegation to apologise to Mr Ndiweni for the destruction of his crops and following that, he released the cattle. Since I knew Dad would still punish me, I continued to evade him for several days. Finally, he mandated Elias to punish me but the punishment was not as severe, thank goodness!

◈ 9 ◈
MY PRIMARY SCHOOL

For my primary education, I went to Nemane SDA which was located in the middle of the Nemane Village about three -quarters of a kilometre from my home.

The Seventh Day Adventist Church ran the school and as a result, religion was emphasised and only baptised church members taught at the school. The church services were held on Saturday in one of the classrooms and it was not compulsory that pupils attend. Pupils like me who were non-Christians only attended church services at our own free will.

It was a typical village school with dusty grounds and inadequate facilities. The school had three classroom blocks and together were in a U-shaped design. In the centre space, we nurtured a drought-resistant lawn, which we only watered every fortnight. It received adequate water during the rain season and that is when it became lush green, providing the school with the much-needed beauty.

Next to the classrooms, grew drought-resistant flowers and they were not that attractive, but at least gave the school some life and they thrived despite little care. During the rainy season, they blossomed and flourished very much.

The blocks consisted of seven classrooms, an office and a storeroom which was also used as a staff room. The school had primary one to primary seven. There were four standard houses and three mud huts for teacher's accommodation.

A borehole that supplied the school with water was about five hundred metres away and it yielded plenty of water. When it broke down an alternative source was an unprotected well, but luckily, we hardly used the well since the borehole rarely broke down.

A small shop that serviced the school sold basic items people could afford. At break-time, all roads led to the borehole, where schoolchildren went to quench their thirst. Only the lucky few went to the shop to buy juice.

Since Nemane had no piped water, we used pit latrines which were shared with teachers, meaning that at weekends or after school, teachers went back to school if they needed the toilet.

The whole village had no proper sanitation and the residents used the bush to relieve themselves. Sometimes that caused a problem for the school as beginners who had not used a pit latrine before were afraid and did not aim properly usually leaving the toilet messy.

We had no janitorial services and it was the responsibility of the pupils to clean the toilets. We took turns to clean them once a week and never had any protective clothing or disinfectant. Amazingly, the outbreak of infectious diseases eluded the school. When the pit latrines filled up they were just sealed and walls demolished.

Among the five surrounding schools, Nemane was the only one with an upper primary class; therefore, children from neighbouring schools came to Nemane for their upper primary.

Some parents staying afar disregarded their local schools and opted for their children to start from primary one at Nemane. The Christian background gave the school a good reputation, as pupils generally behaved well. As there were no boarding facilities, pupils from neighbouring villages walked long distances of up to seven kilometres (four miles).They had to start the walk from their homes very early in the morning for them to reach school in time.

It was a mixed school with an enrolment of about two hundred and fifty pupils and each class had an average of about thirty-five pupils of boys and girls. We sat on wooden benches, which accommodated about three to four pupils and these benches were not very comfortable, as they had no cushions. The teacher had a small wooden table and a chair.

The school offered a variety of academic subjects that included Bible Knowledge, Mathematics, History, English and Geography. It also offered practical subjects like Needlework and Woodwork. The medium of instruction was English although all pupils' first language was vernacular. Pupils did not receive pre-school education and the teachers worked hard to introduce pupils to English and in most cases used the first language to facilitate understanding. To enhance good acquisition of English, it was my schools' policy that all pupils from primary three to communicate in English.

The teachers and prefects enforced this form of communication and anyone who did not adhere to the rules resulted in punishment. Because of deterrent punishment, we made great effort to learn the language faster. It was the norm in my village that anyone who spoke English fluently was educated. This was a motivation for most of us to strive to learn this second language because we aspired to earn respect and classified as learned.

❖10❖
PLAY IN THE NEIGHBOURHOOD

I liked night play and we usually played when we the ploughing season was over. We made use of this precious time as we did not have to wake early to work in the fields. The vast ground behind my homestead was a perfect place for our social catch up. On hot and dry nights, with the bright moonlight, most children in our neighbourhood streamed over to this venue.

We had a variety of games to play but I enjoyed hide and seek mostly. We divided ourselves into pairs, usually of the opposite gender, hid in a secluded bush and the other teams searched. Sometimes the search went on for more than twenty minutes. What fascinated me most was the joyful mood following the discovery of those hiding; we would embrace, laugh and joke too.

We sometimes competed in athletics. Some days, we would play as late as midnight and our parents were not bothered by that.

Due to heat, most insects and reptiles would come out of their hibernation and crawl around especially at night. These creepy crawlies included deadly scorpions, centipedes and sometimes snakes. We played bare footed oblivious of these hazards and over years no was ever scathed.

Occasionally our night play went to the extremes as we ventured far from home into deep thickets to catch birds while they rested. These thickets formed the boundaries between different peoples' fields. At night, those dense forests harboured a variety of flocks of birds. As the forest was so thick, even if the moon shone brightly, the light would not penetrate it. Even during broad daylight, it was daring to penetrate into them.

We walked stealthily among the trees and bushes so as not to disturb the birds. We did that unmindful of the snakes, which might also had been actively preying for birds. In darkness, the birds got disoriented making it easier for us to catch them. That would be delicacy the next day for our meal.

❖11❖
OUR NEIGHBOUR'S SAVAGE REVENGE

I will never forget this very strange, nerve racking and unbelievable incident. One night our cattle broke out of the kraal undetected until the next morning. After the ploughing season, we were generally more relaxed and enjoyed our sleep waking up well after sunrise. My Mum nonetheless was always an early bird.

"Jabu...Jabulani!" Mum called with a distressed voice. With no response my mum switched to calling my elder brother, "Elias, Elias!"

Her second distress call signalled urgent response and without further ado, we responded. We quickly flung off our blankets, dressed up in seconds, and dashed out towards her. That alarming call did not only draw Elias and Jabulani's attention, but the whole family.

"What's the problem, Mum?" Elias enquired

"The cattle...are...gone," she responded in a shaky voice.

We cast our eyes onto the kraal and we were shocked to see it empty. Jabulani checked to see if someone had deliberately let the cattle loose, but the overwhelming evidence showed the cattle had forced themselves out.

We tracked them there and then with all the boys in the family involved. We followed their trail up to a point where it seemed the herd had split into two groups. Some proceeded to the pastures and others to Mr Ncube's millet field. At Mr Ncube's field, the cattle were not there but we were dismayed by the extensive and shocking destruction caused by the herd. A horrible cold chill ran down my spine at the thought of how Ncube would react to the devastation of his field.

Mr Ncube had already impounded them and as the custom was; my parents were to send a delegation to Mr Ncube to apologise. It was his prerogative to accept or reject it and if he rejected it, customarily he would ask for compensation from my Dad. Many a times the offended person would accept the apology.

My Dad was not around, he had gone to visit my uncle who lived miles away and that meant our mothers had to make a decision. Our mothers and brothers therefore convened and discussed at length of whom they would send to convey our profound apology to Ncube. While debating the way forward, little did we know that Ncube had already resolved on the course of action to take! He had decided to do something out of the norm-to attack my Dad.

Ncube had to brace himself for a tough battle because he knew my Dad would overpower him, as my Dad was a former amateur boxer. He had a stint in that field during his stay in South Africa. Mum told us that years back, a group of nine men attacked him and the fight was not over cattle, but a social issue. My Dad defeated them and as a result, everyone in the village became afraid of him. I presume it still lingered in Mr Ncube's memory. In spite of his ability to box, Dad was civil and never involved himself in brawls and even under the influence of beer he controlled himself.

While we still gathered mapping out strategies to appease Ncube and recover the cattle, what followed shocked us. Ncube and his six brothers had besieged our homestead and surrounded us.

"Where is he?" Ncube asked shoving us back and forward.

"Whom...do you... want?" Mum stammered.

"Woman, where is your husband? We'll kill him!" the man shouted brandishing his axe.

They came armed to teeth with axes, spears and knobkerries and were in a terrible mood, their sight terrified us. My heart raced seeing we were no match for them.

"Maye babo… Maye babo!" Mum screamed. "Please forgive us!" She pleaded for mercy.

The men were not in a compromising mood as they ransacked all the huts hunting for my Dad and calling for his head. After a thorough and vigorous search, they interrogated us again.

"You're hiding him," fumed Mr Ncube. "Anyway, here is his heir. He'll pay for his father's sins!" Ncube swore as he approached Elias.

Elias was sitting on a wooden stool next to one of the huts and he never attempted to escape as the drama that was unfolding had taken him by surprise. He just froze and could not utter a word or even plead for mercy.

As Ncube drew closer to him, he drew his axe and aimed at Elias's head, trying to cut it into half. Instinctively, Elias moved his head slightly and the axe made a big cut on his cheek. Elias immediately collapsed as he bled profusely. We were all numb with shock thinking Elias was dead. Ncube and his accomplices must have thought they had killed him instantly because after that they made off.

Mum clutched her head with both arms and started screaming again, "Oh, my son is dead! " As she cried, she moved closer to my butchered brother. Her screaming attracted our neighbours' attention and by the time they came, Elias had regained consciousness. The adults applied traditional medicine to his gaping wound.

When the situation became calm, we sent a delegation to Ncube to recover the cattle and found that he had already released them. Ncube's bizarre and macabre behaviour was just unbelievable. Never before in the village history had callous action like that been witnessed, particularly involving an innocent boy.

When my Dad returned the following day, my Mum gave him time to settle before she broke the sad news to him. My Dad's other two wives were there as well.

"Elias is not very well," Mum, said introducing the subject to Dad.

"Did you give him some medicine?"

"Yes we did."

"What's troubling him?"

"Tom Ncube, our neighbour, is the cause of all this."

"Did he beat him for letting the cattle go astray?"

"Yes, he did."

"Then, there's no problem with that," Dad scoffed.

"There is a serious problem because what transpired is unbelievable."

"What is it?" Dad asked as he gazed straight at my mother's eyes.

"He cut him on the face with an axe."

"What?" My father asked with a fuming voice.

"He wanted to decapitate him but missed. You were the target," Mum said with a quivering voice overcome by emotions.

After a pause she continued, "He was accompanied by his six brothers, all armed with dangerous weapons like axes."

You should have seen Dad's reaction to that shocker. He immediately started sweating; his respirations were deep and very audible and anyone could have guessed what was going to follow.

"Ncube will know who I am! I'll fix his crazy head!" Dad raged as he prepared to retaliate at Ncube and his accomplices.

"Please don't!" My Mum and my Dad's other wives pleaded.

He continued fuming, threatening, and the family persisted, pleading with him until he was calm. Although he changed his mind, he swore to punish Ncube one day.

Elias never went to the hospital but was treated at home with traditional medicine. Such incidents were never reported to the police. As the injury was extensive and compounded with poor management, my brother still bears that scar today.

MY COMMUNITY'S VIEW OF THE DEAD

Apart from teachers and very few people who were Christians, the majority of people in the community believed in ancestral worship. They feared the dead, as they believed that upon death, one's spirit joined the gods and became part of them. They harboured the idea that a person's spirit would protect the family.

The ancestral worshippers appeased the spirits from time to time and the family chose a black ox that would represent the ancestral spirits. This ox got a lot of respect and almost treated like a living being. It was exempt from pulling a plough or a scotch-carts and it was taboo to whip it.

During the rituals, the family would talk to the ox as if they were conversing with a late somebody and addressed it as respected member of family calling it ' Grandfather'. The ceremony would take place after brewing beer with all members of the family present, surrounding the selected ox sprinkling it with beer in the process. The family narrated its challenges and illnesses to the ox so that it relays the message to the gods. The leftover beer will be for the consumption of the family.

Like many others my family firmly believed in traditional worship. From a very tender age, I was somehow sceptical about this belief. I complied to the demands and expectations of my family but with a strong conviction that everything was superstition. I constantly had endless questions of how an ox could be a messenger to the gods to carry out such a noble role.

Whenever drought loomed and it threatened both people and livestock, the chief called all villagers to discuss the way forward. All men and boys in the area would go around the bush destroying everything they believed hindered rainfall. They killed unusual snakes and destroyed deserted birds' nests. They cut down all trees suspected to have been struck by lightning the previous season. They also demolished any abandoned homes. That was ritual cleansing in line with their beliefs.

Sometimes the rains fell after such performances and people strongly believed their gods had accepted their efforts. When that step failed, they tried other options.

The elders of the community selected a few elderly women and men to go to Njelele; a place they believed was sacred. They were to plead with the gods to bring them rains. Njelele is a unique mountain located in Matobo district, one hundred and sixty kilometres (hundred miles) away from my village. At that place, those elderly people appeased the spirits with beer and selected presents.

When the rains fell after the ceremony, the community became exceedingly happy, but if it failed, counter accusations followed. They believed the gods disapproved some of the delegates. They initiated further efforts to satisfy the gods and if it still failed, it was then that they gave up and remained optimistic for the next rain season.

Under normal circumstances, the ploughing season ran from November to January. Our fields covered a very extensive area, the farming method we used was subsistence, and consequently it compromised quality and quantity. My parents believed that the larger the area, the more production. Lack of farming methods and resources hampered bumper harvests in the expense of hard labour put in.

Since we used ox-drawn ploughs, we covered less area than using a tractor. Farming also heavily depended on erratic rainfall. Due to the use of slow tilling methods, the land dried up before we covered the whole area and we could not plough the entire field.

Our parents knew nothing about crop rotation that could have enhanced fertility. They grew the same crop in the same place year after year. They did not fertilise the land using manure due to ignorance. The soils in our area, which were sandy, also contributed to the poor harvests.

We did not sow seeds row by row but scattered them and that method had many disadvantages because it left some seeds exposed. Either birds picked them or the sun scorched them. The plough also buried some seeds deep down and those had no chance to germinate. Another hitch was that we did not buy graded seeds but used poor quality ones that had poor yields.

When sowing seeds, we mixed various crops, for example, millet, maize and groundnuts. That affected crops growth because they competed for food as different crops need different nutrients and that farming method led to crop failure.

We could not cope with cultivating crops in time because the fields were too big. To make matters worse, we did that manually which meant we needed more time with only women and girls to do that task. Delayed weeding resulted in crops competing with weeds for growth and that affected them resulting in poor yields and harvests. In some cases, there was poor rainfall that worsened the situation.

My Dad had his own field that was smaller than for our mothers'. That field had clay soils that were good for crops. His style of farming was more intensive and productive. He added manure to it biennially with all manure from the kraals. He used better methods of farming in his field and we did not scatter the seeds but sowed them row by row. We sowed each type of crop in its section. When cultivating, we used an ox-drawn cultivator instead of using manual hoes. The field had no tree stumps as compared to our mothers' fields. I do not know why they practised different farming methods.

His field was more productive compared to our mothers' fields. Collectively what our mothers produced in their vast fields almost equalled the produce from my Dad's field. The three family units shared the produce from my father's field and when that food got finished, each family unit fended for its self.

❖13❖
MOVING HOME

On one instance, my Dad was away from home for almost a week and that got me worried. He used to take these trips away from home but we all knew where he was. This prompted me to approach my Mum to ask about his whereabouts because I suspected that she knew something about it.

"Mum, where is Dad?" I probed.

"Why are you nosey? It's none of your business."

"I'm sorry, Mum," I responded and walked away.

Two weeks passed by and Dad was nowhere to be seen. During the third week, he came back home, fit and sound.

When I saw Dad arrive, I did not run to meet and hug him because it was not our custom. When an adult like our Dad arrived from a visit, we only greeted them after allowing them settle down and we even kept our distance from him. That was our way of life; it was not out of fear but respect.

After a good rest, Dad called my Mum and his other wives for a private talk. They stayed in that hut for a long time and we only overheard laughter, ululations and clapping of hands. When they emerged from the hut, they were all in high spirits and on cloud nine.

They dispersed and went to their various kitchens. Mum called me and obviously, curiosity was killing me.

"Isn't that you wanted to know where your Dad had gone?" She asked beaming a broad smile.

"Oh yes, Mum." I could not wait for her to break the ice.

She related the whole matter from the time Dad left up to that day's news. She said Dad had decided to relocate the family from Nemane to Vulashaba, a place that was about one hundred and twenty-three kilometres (seventy-seven miles) away. It was at the far end to the north of Tsholotsho and was a very fertile place in which from year after year farmers had a bumper harvest. The news was exciting and exhilarating and elevated the spirits of the entire family.

I was also very happy and looked forward to seeing Vulashaba. The idea of transferring to a new school and meeting new teachers aroused my thoughts to great heights. I did not bother leaving my current friends as the thought of the new place had captured me.

The family had to move before the rainy season commenced as a lot of work waited the family to make this new home habitable. This included clearing the bush for the homestead and the fields. We had to erect new structures before rains started because it would be impossible to build under the rainy conditions.

My Dad, our mothers and all older siblings except for all school going children went ahead to do the preparations. The relocation took place during the school term and it was sensible for us to remain to complete the term's work. Two of our grown-up sisters who had completed school remained with us to cater for our welfare during the absence of our parents.

My family moved from Nemane to Vulashaba using ox-drawn

carts to ferry our property. My Dad had hired one cart from Vulashaba to help carry some of the load and act as a guide. They left with livestock as well and it meant a bit of a holiday for us because we were not going to herd cattle. We spent our time playing with our friends.

Due to the mode of removal transport, the journey was long and laborious, taking almost a week to reach their destination. They had various stopovers to rest as well as to allow the livestock to feed.

For three months, we stayed at Nemane while our parents settled in Vulashaba and during this period we never heard anything from them, as there was no means of communication. Time seemed to drag on for the school holidays to start as I missed my Mum and the rest of the family that went ahead.

At the end of the year I passed very well, I scored the highest in my class. I was very happy, as that would have given me a good footing at my new school.

The day before we left, I went around the village, bidding farewell to my friends and the prospect of separation overwhelmed us but we consoled each other by promising to communicate through letters.

❖14❖
MY FIRST VISIT TO VULASHABA

The following morning we woke up very early to catch up the bus and in no time, it arrived. As I went into the bus, I took the last glance of the village I was born in, I felt gloomy to think I would never see my friends again. That feeling almost brought me to tears.

In about two hours, we were in Tsholotsho Business Centre, we and other passengers alighted to get a connection bus. The few that remained in were probably proceeding to Bulawayo city.

It did not take long before our next bus arrived and we boarded. I knew the journey would take long since Vulashaba was further than Nemane, I braced myself, and I perched in a good seat for the long journey ahead.

Apart from my family members, the rest of the passengers were strangers and the behaviour of some was somehow strange. So early in the morning they were gulping beer and I assumed we were in for a shock.

The bus sped along dusty, rough and bumpy road as it tried to cover the long distance that lay ahead. As the bus hit each bump, I felt the stress going up my spine.

The bad state of the road combined with the smell of diesel, did not augur well with me as it made me feel sick. Without further warning, I threw up all the food I had eaten that morning and unfortunately, I messed the woman who sat beside me. Although she did not complain, I felt very bad about it and I was so embarrassed. After sickness, the disturbing feelings gradually subsided and I could now stand the bumpy road and the smell of diesel.

It was not long before the effects of alcohol started showing in those passengers that were drinking as they sang and danced in an uncontrolled manner. One of them paced up and down the bus aisle disturbing other passengers. In my lifetime, I had never seen adults who behaved as they did. Despite all that, I enjoyed the scenery outside; the thick forest with long dry grass was a spectacular scene. The forests of Vulashaba were denser compared to those of Nemane and since it was winter and I could imagine how the area looked like in summer.

The bus had several stops before we reached our destination late in the afternoon. The weather at Mtshwayeli Village was beautiful with cool air blowing across the area. Some people were lingering at the bus stop and we learnt that some had come to meet their loved ones whereas the rest had come to while away time. Among the crowd were our two brothers, Sfa and Jabulani, who had come to meet us. The reunion was ecstatic. Never before had we separated that long.

We made our way home chatting in excitement, but however in no time, sandy soils silenced us as it become more difficult to walk faster. We removed our shoes because sand was getting in them and it was irritating. Our brothers explained that the excessive sand was the reason why the bus did not proceed to Vulashaba. We wondered how the thick vegetation thrived so well in sandy soils.

By sunset, we had reached our new homestead and the whole family rushed to meet us as we approached. They were in a happy mood and this created commotion as we hugged and welcomed each other.

"Hello, Atra! You have grown so tall. It's surprising the difference three months can make!" My father's third wife remarked.

"Is that so, Mum? Thank you. I missed you so much." Atra responded to her mother's compliments.

The whole family sat down and related to each other its experiences. Dad joined us and it was happy moment for the family.

When I casted my eyes around, the construction of huts was complete and they had maintained the setup which was a replica of the Nemane one. My mother's huts were still in the centre of the home and the only difference was that the huts were roomy and more beautiful. The amount of work done in three months was just unbelievable; the family deserved a pat on their backs. I looked forward to meeting new friends and to enjoying my stay. I eagerly waited to explore those thick forests.

During suppertime, I realised a new and interesting development – the three family units cooked and dined together. When an opportunity arose, I approached Mum for an explanation about the new status quo.

"Mum, how come we cook and dine together?" I quizzed. After a breather I continued, "Is it going to be the trend now?"

"Your Dad decided that we cook together." She replied. Placing her right hand on my shoulder, she went on, "Don't worry, food is in abundance here."

"I think it's a good idea," I commented.

"So do I," Mum smiled.

We also had a new set up for the bedrooms since I did not share the bedroom with Elias and Jabulani anymore, but with other boys of my age. Some of my brothers had immigrated to South Africa. Those were Elias, Pedias, Nelson and Edmond, Jabulani remained at home. I found it as a brilliant idea for the same age siblings to share bedrooms as we had a lot in common. Before we went to bed, our elder brothers reminded us that we should stand our ground when local boys try to bully us and we pledged not to disappoint them.

❖ 15 ❖
MY FIRST EXPERIENCES IN VULASHABA

Very early in the morning, before breakfast, we went to the fields to check if they were ready for ploughing. The work done was impressive as the fields were ready.

The fields were in virgin land that was very fertile with a combination of sandy red and clay soils. Basing from our little knowledge in farming, we could forecast a bumper harvest.

After exploring the fields, we had our questions answered by the status quo then we made our way back home. We also realised that the homesteads were isolated, a sign that the area was sparsely populated. Our immediate neighbour was Mr Sithole and his homestead was very close to ours.

When we arrived home, some neighbours had come to welcome us. I had always thought my family was one of the least privileged but when I saw some of the children brought by our neighbours, I had second thoughts. They still wore 'ibhetshu', the traditional gear I wore years back before I even started school. The children were dirty also, but in spite of their appearances, they were welcoming and sociable.

Vulashaba village had water problems and the only source of water was a borehole in the area, which was about two kilometres (one mile) away from our homestead. The path to that borehole was sandy making it impossible to walk carrying a bucket of water and therefore collected water in big drums using ox-drawn carts.

Sandy paths and the distant borehole was not the only snag. The borehole itself was heavy to draw water as it took about ten minutes for four to five people to collectively pump water to fill a twenty-litre can.

The few water holes in the area dried up in summer, we had an arduous task to pump the water manually for our livestock. The water problem made me to become doubtful about Vulashaba being a better alternative for us.

We commenced ploughing and thankfully, the fields were not as large as the Nemane ones. We had also improved on our farming methods; instead of scattering, we sowed the seeds row by row. We also majored in maize growing, as the soils were favourable for that crop. We had a very good and healthy crop that promised a bumper harvest, a sure sign that Nemane's poor harvests would be history.

Time moved fast and soon schools were to open. I had acclimatised well and had begun to enjoy life there and I looked forward to starting my primary three in a new school. Eight of us in my family were to attend school.

I learnt that Mlevu School was about fifteen kilometres (nine miles) away and I wondered how we would be getting there since there was no transport system linking the two places. Our parents suggested that we would board in the village next to the school. We were not going to stay in one place but allocated to different homes. That was a bitter pill to swallow – to imagine staying with strangers with no other family member made my heart to sink.

Flash memories of Nemane School that was only a stone's throw from my home filled my head. I recalled the difficulties faced by children who came from afar away to attend school at Nemane. I consoled myself that things would work out in a positive way.

Our parents established contacts where we were going to stay and some of them were our distant relatives; we had never met them before. The only positive aspect was that we would visit home every weekend.

My Dad went to the school to register us and the teacher on duty did not have full details as the head of the school was on holiday. All he told him was that the school would welcome to enrol us all and asked him to return a week before schools started to complete the registration forms.

Days moved quickly and soon Dad returned to the school. I was very anxious to know the outcome of his trip.

"How is my new school, dad?" I asked.

"The school looks good, but unfortunately there is no place for you," he replied. "They do not have a primary three class this year."

His reply devastated me; I could not believe or understand what he meant and I sought for further clarification.

"What do you mean? Will I not go to school anymore?" I asked with a quivering voice, tears rolling down my cheeks.

"There is no way you can go to that school."

His words were shattering and the world seemed to have turned upside down for me. What quickly flashed into my mind was that I would become a permanent herd boy and all my aspirations transcended to zero. All I could do was just to cry.

"The option is to repeat year two." My father explained.

"No... I passed, it's unfair!" I sobbed bitterly.

"The other alternative is going back to Nemane," Dad suggested and that was like adding salt to an injury. I could not tolerate going back to Nemane on my own.

"Dad I gather there is another school seven kilometres further from that school. Why don't I go to that school?" I pleaded with him.

"It's not feasible. There is no one we know there. If you don't want then you'll repeat year two," Dad concluded and left for the fields.

As soon as he left, Tennyson came to me. He also looked worried.

"What will you do then? Will you go back to Nemane or repeat primary two?" Tennyson quizzed.

"I am really in a dilemma as none of the options is good. What do you think?" I enquired.

We talked at length and finally reached a compromise that returning to Nemane would be a better option. Tennyson comforted me in that I was in a better position than them who were going to reside with unknown relatives. I gradually came to terms with that because I had no better solution and more so I wanted to proceed with my education.

I hated the idea of going back to my former school as I found it embarrassing to go back after I bade farewell to my friends only a few weeks ago. Another disturbing factor was the long distance from my family, which meant I would spend almost four months away from them.

In Nemane, I would stay with my sister, Elizabeth, who was married and her homestead was only a kilometre away from our former home. She got married when I was too young and I had not bonded with her very much. To make matters worse she was married in an extended family where she resided with her in-laws. I wondered how I would fit into that family. I comforted myself that since she was my blood sister, there was no way she would mistreat me.

Those days there were no means of communication like telephones. Letters also took ages before reaching their destination and so my sister would only know of my predicament when I got there. Anyway, formalities were not very much of an issue because those days children were an asset. By staying with my sister and her family, they would treat me like their own child. I would take part in all family chores like herding cattle and ploughing. Culturally, there was no way my sister would shun me.

Time to return to Nemane soon arrived, I bid farewell to my family and left by bus. I was sad; however, I had no choice. I tried hard to accept that and forged ahead.

On my way, I kept on pondering why it became me and I thought I must be the most unfortunate person. Amidst that I consoled myself that the various aspirations I had, could only be realised through completing my education. That thought encouraged me and made me resilient.

❖16❖
I JOIN MY SISTER'S FAMILY

By sunset, I arrived at Nemane and the weather was wonderful with a beautiful typical African sunset with cool breeze blowing across the village. The early rains had completely transformed the surrounding vegetation and every plant had sprung back to life. As there were few people at the bus station, I quickly made my way to my sister's homestead, which was not very far-off.

As I approached the home, I could see my sister sitting next to her hut, but she did not see me, as she seemed engrossed in her thoughts. As she stretched herself, she caught sight of me, but she was not excited as she probably anticipated I brought bad news.

"Hello Calvin. I didn't expect to see you so soon?"

"Is everything alright?" She asked.

"Oh, yes, "I quickly allayed her anxiety.

"Ah! What a relief! I thought you brought sad news." She breathed a sigh of relief and then welcomed me formally.

I then related why I had come and she was in agreement with my decision. We chatted for a long time before the other members of her family joined in. Everyone welcomed me well and my sister then explained why I had come and no one in her family objected.

Elizabeth also stayed with her brother-in-law, John, who was my age mate. Of all the people in my sister's family, John was the most excited knowing I would be his companion and also assist him with herding cattle.

John took me around to their kraal to show me the herd of cattle and we chatted spontaneously. He related to me some issues he encountered while herding cattle and expressed his profound joy that at last he had someone to work with.

"You also have a big herd of cattle. What's the name of that bull?"

"It's called 'Jealous'. We gave it that name because it does not entertain other bulls mingling with our herd."

After viewing the cattle, we continued with our conversation as we made our way back to the homestead sharing matters boys would discuss on their own.

The Gumbo family were devout Christians and attended the local church that ran the school. My sister's parents-in law were 'elders' in the church. The only non-Christian was MaNdebele, the wife of Richard's younger brother who worked in South Africa. With me joining the family, another non- believer was added.

This family had adequate meals and everyone seemed happy. We did not scramble for food because the family was an average one with nine people compared to my family, which was far too big.

John had a bed of his own which we were going to share but I reasoned with John to let me sleep on the floor as I had never in my life slept in a bed . John assured me of the comfort and safety I could enjoy; I finally agreed to join him. As you imagine that was a nightmare to me as I was very scared. Thrice in my sleep I nearly fell off the bed and at one point my legs dangled to the floor.

Instead of being peaceful, the night was uncomfortable and bizarre.

The following morning I put on my school uniform and I went to school. When I arrived, I proceeded straight to the headmaster's office wondering how he would receive me. After knocking at the door, he indicated that I should enter the office.

"Why are back? Didn't you get a transfer letter?" the headmaster asked.

"I did, but…there're problems," I said, as I stammered.

"What problems?" He continued to ask.

I explained the circumstances surrounding my coming and he then welcomed me back. He expressed that since I had no behavioural problems and generally, a hard worker they would gladly accept me back. He showed me my new class and asked me to go and call my teacher.

After relaying the message, the teacher and I went to the headmaster's office. The headmaster narrated to him the situation and after that together with the teacher, I went to join the other pupils.

As I entered the classroom, all faces turned on me and I knew I had many questions to answer. During break time, all curious ones came, encircled me, and asked why I had come back. They also wanted to hear about Vulashaba. Mixed reactions flared up though as those I had outclassed the previous term did not like my return. My best friends expressed the pleasure of my returning.

❖17❖
MY ENCOUNTER WITH A BULLY (11 YEARS OLD)

After school, I went back to my new residence, quickly had my lunch and then joined the rest of the family for the afternoon activities. Thank goodness, they were no different from the ones I performed in my family. It was mainly looking after cattle and I therefore, never struggled to carry them out.

Both my sister's parents- in-law were hard working especially her father- in- law, Mr Gumbo, woke up early in the morning and went to the fields with us. He worked as hard as everyone did. He was approachable and had a pleasant manner. Unlike most men of his era, we shared jokes with him.

We used to herd cattle with John and his cousin Robbie who stayed not very far. During my first few days, I noticed that John and Robbie were cowards. Jim, one of the local boys, took that as a weakness and always bullied them.

"Come here, John!" Jim commanded.

Without hesitation, John hastily walked towards Jim. I just watched motionless.

"John, you must run when I call you. I'm the king of the bush!" The bully boasted.

It was at that juncture that John ran to meet the boss. He looked stocky, heavily built and older. Jim looked pleased by what he did to John.

"Who is that stubborn boy? You should let him know that I rule the savannah!" He declared as he pointed at me with his index finger.

His reaction bewildered me and I questioned myself what wrong had I done. After all, it was the third time I met him and had not done anything wrong to upset him.

"Come here!" He beckoned me.

Still bemused, all I had to do was to lick my lips, as I did not know what action to take. He made quick steps towards me threatening to beat me up. I looked at him and he was raging with eyes blazing. I thought of taking to my heels, but something in me compelled me to stay put.

Where I came from, nobody ever bullied me. My mother's wise words echoed in my mind. She always emphasised that I should avoid confrontation at all cost. On the other hand, my brother, Jabulani's advice was not to allow myself to be a pushover. Those two parallel advices baffled me; I was at cross roads to make an instant decision. I did not know if any of those decisions would backfire. Finally, I opted for my brother's bold opinion.

As the bully approached me, I was shaking and terrified. I quickly remembered the knife in my pocket. Like all herd boys, I always carried a knife. This was not for sinister purposes but was a handy tool we used a lot in the bush, to curve, for an example a knob carry. Being in a very precarious position, I Instantly drew the knife from my right pocket in readiness to use it. I grabbed him by the collar of his shirt with my left hand and shoved him backwards and forwards. I then lifted my right hand in a bid to tear him apart. At that moment, the bully was petrified. I proceeded with my effort to stab him and unfortunately, due to nervousness I stabbed my left hand instead.

Oh, that was disastrous and I knew I had sold myself to the bully. Quickly I let go and sped off with the bully on hot pursuit heading towards my sister's homestead. Although it was a distance away, I was determined to run for my life.

On the way, I became tired and my legs unable to carry me. My heart began pounding heavily with each pace but I could not stop because the 'beast' was behind and I could hear him panting. He was so daring and very determined to apprehend me and carry out his retribution. I ran for death and life until I reached home. My brother-in law, Richard, was outside and I quickly sought refuge behind him.

"Jim, what are you doing? Don't you see that this boy is younger than you?" Richard shouted as he protected me.

"I'll kill him, he thinks he's smart!" Jim swore in a high-pitched voice.

Jim threatened and muttered disobediently as he went out of the yard. Apparently, Jim was a cousin to Richard, maybe that was why he managed to control him.

After Jim left, Richard asked me what caused the fiasco. I related the whole story from the time he bullied John up to the point I drew a knife.

"That was not a good action to take. Don't you know you could have stabbed him to death?" Richard explained to me the effects of impulsive retaliation.

"I'm sorry, I didn't mean to. He's the one who started and all I did was to defend myself," I tried to justify my course of action.

It was not easy. I had a sleepless night pondering over how I would face Jim. I knew he would keep a grudge and the next time we meet, he would want to settle the score.

I thought of my brother Jabulani who was not an easy nut to crack. Jim behaved that way because there was no one to defend me. That pained me, tears rolled down my cheeks.

The following day together with John, I took the cattle to the pastures. Chills of fear ran down my spine as I thought of Jim again. Though I dreaded going to the pastures, I had already come up with a way to defend myself. I told myself I should never be timid like the hunted, but be bold like a hunter.

The evening before, I had made a spear using a sharpened metal rod. Making it was not a problem since Richard's carpentry shop had all the raw materials I needed. I was determined to defend myself at all costs. I presumed the spear would be advantageous over a knife because of its length. Even if I was fully armed, my intention was not confrontation but self-defence. Naturally, I disliked violence but in order to survive on this occasion, I had to equip myself with this dangerous weapon.

The whole day I had a sense of insecurity fearing Jim would ambush me. Luckily the day was ending and I never saw the 'beast'. At about sunset we drove the cattle back home and about a mile from home, I spotted Jim approaching. He came directly to me armed with a knobkerrie that had a long thick handle. Wild-eyed, he charged like a mad bull, but I remained unperturbed, holding onto my spear with the point down.

"You think you're smart, boy! You'll regret!" Jim threatened as he grabbed me.

He lifted his knobkerrie aiming to hit my head and knock me down. Out of sheer luck I managed to block, it and in the process, I lost grip of the spear. We wrestled onto the ground until Jim fell down helplessly.

I really do not know where I got the courage and strength. I grabbed him by his leg and I began meting out instant justice on him using the stick-end of his knobkerrie. I thrashed him with quick and powerful whips. He could not avoid it, but bellow like an ox on a slaughter.

"Oh! Forgive me. I won't do it again!" He pleaded for mercy.

His screams seemed to stimulate me to bash him incessantly.

"Forgive me please. I... won't do it again!" Jim whimpered with a shrilled voice.

I ignored his pleas and continued to give him severe beating, making him taste his own medicine. At that time, some other herd boys were yelling and urging me to thump him more. The punishment left him with wet pants and multiple bruises.

Henceforth, he regarded me with a high esteem, even John and Robbie got the respect they deserved. Every boy who heard of the incidence treated me with high regard. Despite being a victor, I never bullied or abused anyone.

Time moved so fast, I became used to staying with my sister's family, and I became part of them. All this was due to their hospitality. Richard was a very quiet man who never liked quarrelling, and he even found it hard to discipline his own children. He was a carpenter by profession and had acquired those skills from my father and it was during that time he courted my sister.

He used his skills very well as he made reasonable profits to support his family and buy some sizeable livestock. The local society respected him. During those days, society accorded respect to a man by the size of his herd of cattle.

Although my sister's family was a devout one, they never forced me to go to church. I suppose they respected my beliefs and understood that in Christianity only the willing come.

Consequently, John and I attended church sparingly. However, on their day of worship, no work was carried out within their homestead and even food was prepared a day before.

From my background, we ate meat from animals that died of natural causes but that family did not. MaNdebele and I continued with our beliefs and the family did not shun us. Once a fowl died from snakebite, MaNdebele roasted it, and together we enjoyed it.

I also became used to sleeping in a bed. The separation from my family seemed not to affect me as I continued to excel in my schoolwork.

School term ended and it was time to go to Vulashaba to be with my family. My sister informed me that it was not possible that term end because she had no money for my bus fare. I did not quite agree to that for two reasons. Firstly, my sister's husband, Richard, made lots of money from his small carpentry business and I thought my sister was just mean. Secondly, I suspected she wanted me to continue taking care of the cattle during the holidays. I could not accept her reasons at her words, as I was homesick. After all, I had not enjoyed much at our new place and there was so much for me to see.

That night I went berserk and refused to go to bed. I sat on a rock at the back of my sister's bedroom and screamed continuously. My sister tried to knock sense into my head but I could not give in. Finally, after nagging her so much, she reversed her decision. She promised I would leave the following morning and it is then that I agreed to go to bed.

The next morning I boarded the bus to Vulashaba, very eager to rejoin my family. By late in the evening I had arrived there.

❖18❖
INTERESTING DEVELOPMENTS

My clan welcomed me in a tremendous way that I never doubted that they had missed me. Everyone wanted an update about Nemane. After exhausting the discussions with the family, Tennyson winked at me and we quickly went out as I anticipated he had breaking news to share behind adult's back.

"Guess what?" Tennyson teased.

"What is it?" I responded with a very curious look.

"Guess who could be a new member of the family?" Tennyson persisted with his jigsaw puzzle.

"It's a new baby," I tried to guess.

"No," Tennyson continued with his brainteaser.

"Hey, you're killing me with curiosity, break the ice," I lost patience in guessing.

"Our Dad has married a fourth wife," Tennyson elaborated.

That stunned me and I could not wait any longer to see the revelation.

I quickly went to see and greet her. What a shocker! She was about 18 and coming to marry my father who was in his late fifties.

My Mum and my father's other two wives were in their early fifties. Regardless of her age, culturally, my other mothers were to treat her as their equally and we had to bestow her full respect. In short, treat her as our mum.

I also noticed that Jabulani was not at home and I quickly enquired about his whereabouts. I suspected he had not gone far and would return soon.

"Jabulani left three months ago," Mum told me.

"Where did he go to?" I asked in amazement.

"He's now working in South Africa."

"Is that so?" I gaped.

"If you don't believe me, I can give you his letter," she said as she stood up to collect it from her bedroom.

I read it slowly and it confirmed what Mum had just told me. In the letter, he narrated of his journey. He had travelled with our cousin, Dallas and some of the contents were astonishing.

Because most of their journey was on foot, it took them three weeks. What stunned me most was when they strayed into Kruger National Game Park. Inevitably, they came face to face with the big five.

They spent nights on treetops and used belts to secure themselves. He described the nights as horrible. There was one night that was outrageous and unbearable because under the tree, there were three lions roaring and making all efforts to pounce on them. The lions roared in an effort to intimidate them and if by chance one of them dropped, he would have been a meal for those lions. Fright bemused and benumbed them. The two never expected to survive that night as one lioness even attempted to climb up the tree. All they could do was to hold onto their dear lives.

At daybreak, the lions gave up and dispersed. What a relief!

They thanked their ancestors for spiritual protection. After making sure the lions had vanished, they quickly ran for dear life. Fortunately, they managed to go through the game park and in a few days, they were in Johannesburg.

"Woo ... Mum, Johannesburg is not for me! I'm not prepared to sacrifice my precious life for that!" I commented after reading that moving letter. Mum also echoed my sentiments and encouraged me not to.

From the meal I had that evening, I deduced that the fields did extremely well. I became eager to visit the fields the first thing in morning.

In the morning, I had breakfast served by Mum. Unexpectedly, she also served me tea. I could not help asking for an explanation.

"How come we also take tea now?" I enquired.

"Ah, our fields are doing so well and we've started selling the produce."

"At least we get so much even to afford luxury," I marvelled.

"Yes, my son, tea is now for everyone in the family."

I now really appreciated my parent's move to Vulashaba. After breakfast, I made my way to the fields accompanied by Tennyson and what I saw gratified me, the fields were flourishing and a bumper harvest imminent. This confirmed that the poor harvests we experienced at Nemane would soon be history.

As the days went by, I became used to the Vulashaba inhabitants and their way of life. Apparently, they did not value education as none of their children attended school. The entire population was illiterate. My siblings were the only ones who were in school. They could not comprehend why I had to go to all the way to Nemane just to attend school. It just did not make sense. This was bound to have a knock on effect on our family's quest for further education.

Even so, they regarded us as an enlightened family as we could read and write. In addition, our large herd of cattle made us gain the villagers' respect. Every elderly person wished their sons or daughters to get married within our family unlike in Nemane where somehow people despised us.

It was the norm for adults to arrange marriages for their daughters in that community. The daughters were to comply without objection. Men with a large herd of cattle were in a good position to marry younger wives. It is how my Dad acquired his fourth wife. He gave her family three cows as a token of appreciation. In the African tradition, a man is required to pay dowry before marrying a girl.

One thing those villagers enjoyed most was holding parties and these parties attracted both the young and the old. The organiser brewed beer and cooked food for sale. Those bashes were uncivilised and notorious for high crime rate. I also found myself hooked up in them.

At those parties, they played a gramophone. If any one wanted to dance his favourite song, he had to pay for that chance. Only the person who paid the stipulated amount could dance. The parties jammed the whole night and people danced, drunk beer and sometimes betted on cards.

A sour incident occurred during one of those parties. It involved some elderly men who had a betting school at a beer drinking spot. They were drunk and it would appear beer ruined and incapacitated their minds. The kraal head was also part of the group and yet he had to be exemplary in the community.

Those men bet with their hard-earned cash hoping to multiply it. In most cases, they ended up losing everything. This created friction between the losers and their spouses.

Before the game was over, it was mandatory for the winner to offer the losers a free bet. This will be the loser's final hope to turn the tables and recover their lost cash. If they still lost then, the winner had the right to end the game and declare himself the ultimate winner.

Moyo was one of the well-known gamblers. After he had sold his large ox, he went straight to the betting school with the hope to multiply his cash. Unfortunately, luck did not smile on him that day as he lost all his hard-earned cash.

Ncube also lost cash he received after selling his farm produce. He no longer had a lifeline to recover his money since the winner; Dewa had already given him his free bet. All he had to do was to walk away in despair and think of a way he would explain the loss to his wife. According to the rules of the game, the money now belonged to Dewa. Ncube would not take that. However, Moyo was still to get his free bet and he was very optimistic that slim chance would rekindle his chances to regain his lost cash.

"Dewa, I want my money back! I didn't sell my corn for your benefit," Ncube said fuming for his lost cash.

"You must be joking! I didn't force you into this game." Dewa said stating his stance. "Just as I do, you know the rules of this game. The money belongs to me now!"

That enraged Ncube, in a twinkling of an eye Ncube picked up a wooden stool, and struck Dewa on the head. Dewa fell down and became unconscious. Everyone was speechless and the first person to have courage to talk was Moyo.

"Dewa has died before offering me a free bet. Who will offer me that last chance to help me recover back my money," Moyo said as he moaned for his lost chance.

His utterances amazed everyone who witnessed that callous incident. Moyo, a respected kraal head, moaned for money instead of sympathising with Dewa.

There was no control at those parties as even young people drank the African brew at liberty. The owner of the party did not care, as all he wanted was money. People who had taken the traditional beer seemed to be in high spirits and this influenced me to taste it. After all, I also appeared stupid not to drink because most boys were drinking. My parents did not object, but instead, encouraged us.

Taking beer was as if one had attained a hero status and it would be the talk of the family. Thankfully, I did not like the taste of beer and the behaviour of people after drinking.

There were many nasty squabbles during those parties. Some people lost their teeth and others sustained life threatening stab wounds. Incidents like those never reached the police because the people involved would solve the matter amicably among themselves. They would attribute the actions to beer. Sometimes they would comment that the beer was well brewed hence it intoxicated them badly. That also did not amuse me and contributed to my abrupt decision to quit partying and drinking.

"Helele, Helele!" my Mum and my Dad's other wives would break into songs on their way back from a drinking spot.

Under normal circumstances my Mum and my Dad's other wives could fight for favours from my Dad but drinking together seemed to bind them because they could sing and dance peacefully.

Vulashaba was only a few kilometres away from Hwange National Park, one of the world's largest game parks. A home to all the dangerous animals found in Africa including the big five. The animals often broke the fence and strayed to our village with the lions being the most culprits. We were wary of their presence as they could attack our livestock or us. On two occasions, they killed two of our cows.

Elephants were also a menace because they caused a great deal of destruction in the fields. Villagers often reported the incidents to the local district offices that sent game rangers to scare them with gunfire. Elephants like melons a lot and it was advisable never to keep melons in the compound.

I heard of an incidence that occurred while I was at Nemane. A certain man who slept in an incomplete hut structure stored his melons there. The structure was made of logs leaving spaces in between them and it was still in the process of completion by sealing it with mud.

One night a lone elephant wandered into the man's compound as the man was asleep. The smell of the melons drew the elephant to the incomplete structure.

The elephant tried to retrieve the melons by squeezing its trunk on the empty space between the logs. The man panicked seeing the trunk in the hut and he thought of saving himself. He took an axe and aimed at its trunk in the hope of punishing the elephant. Taking into consideration the toughness of the trunk, I really wonder what his aim was. Maybe it was an impulsive action to scare the elephant away. Whatever his motives were, his actions were weird and dangerous.

The impact of the axe provoked the elephant and it became incensed and ran amok. It destroyed that structure and the man survived by a whisker. He ran under the cover of darkness to his neighbours for refuge. That story made me scared of Vulashaba.

I continued with my daily duties like herding cattle while on holiday. I discovered that the place was far richer in wild fruits than Nemane.

On some occasions, we could hear lions roaring and that scared both the cattle and us. Herding cattle turned out to be dangerous and one needed to be vigilant for oneself and for the livestock.

From time to time, we took the cattle for dipping. The dip tank was very far away and to get there in time, we had to leave home before dawn and came back at dusk. What I never liked was driving the cattle in deep forests in the dark. Each time we moved in darkness anything could have happened to us. The dangerous wild animals are usually active by then. That continued to haunt me each time we went to the dipping post. I sometimes wonder how we survived even injuries from thorns and so on.

I stayed in Vulashaba throughout the entire holiday and returned to Nemane two days before schools commenced.

❖19❖
MY BAD INFLUENCE

At Nemane, I found that my sister's fields were flourishing too but not to match the Vulashaba ones.

Time moved fast and soon harvest was over. After harvest, boys normally went around the field scouting for left over corn. John and I started our rounds collecting corn for our benefit. This corn was of poor quality and we sold it to the miller for meagre cents. With the cash, I bought myself a pair of pants and a vest. Imagine! That was the first time I wore a vest and an under pant.

At night, the Gumbos never allowed evening plays as they thought that was unsafe. That never went down well with me, but I had to oblige. As time elapsed, I developed naughty tactics and influenced John so we could sneak away together. I could not resist the temptation to play because other children's yells motivated me. Since I had an experience of night plays when I stayed with my family, I knew the great fun we missed. We normally had dinner late in the evening and after that, we remained in the kitchen chatting until late at night. Each time after dinner, we pretended to be tired and slumbered in the kitchen.

"Hey boys, this is not your bedroom, if you feel like sleeping, go to bed," Richard would usually say. We would then bid the rest of the family goodnight and go to our bedroom. Little did the family know we had hatched a plan?

"Ah! John, we conned them," I said in a happy mood.

"Oh yes, we're geniuses," John concurred.

We quickly sneaked out to join other children at play. These children knew about the Gumbo family's policy. They probed us to tell them how we made it and we quickly let the cat out of the bag. We begged them not to tell anyone our secret. Sometimes we went to play miles away from home.

Our crafty sneaking went on for a long time undetected. One day it dawned on us that what we were doing was wrong and speculated on the risks that we could encounter. We reversed our decision and stopped our illegal plays before we were caught red handed.

Soon school term ended and this time I had a lifetime opportunity to visit my sister Sophie in the city. Sophie had remarried and her life seemed to have improved. She had three more children from her new marriage. However, Forester and Never continued to live with my Mum. They were now somehow her adopted children and they identified her as their Mum instead of grandma.

The impending visit excited me and I could not wait. I even forgot about the family in Vulashaba. I could not resist telling my friends about my looming trip and they were stunned to hear that.

Bulawayo is a large city and located about one hundred and twenty-three kilometres (seventy-six miles) away from Nemane. I visited the city once with Mum when I was very young and I could not remember a thing about the city. I was just like someone who had never been there, hence the curiosity. I could only vividly remember one incident that occurred during that visit. A Good Samaritan had offered me a bottle of fanta juice and we were sitting outside in a veranda. I had just taken a sip of the drink, when I accidentally dropped the bottle onto the concrete floor, and it broke.

I was very sad because I had just tasted its sweetness. I looked at the broken bottle with great loss and cried bitterly because that was the first time I tasted a fanta drink. I hoped by crying I would get another offer but unfortunately, that was never so.

I knew going to the city would be a time to enjoy for me; moreover, there were no cattle to herd or work in the fields. I waited in great anticipation for what I termed my first holiday ever. I knew nothing about television then and so I could not imagine how a city looked like.

❖❖ 20 ❖❖
MY FIRST VISIT TO A CITY (12 YEARS OLD)

I woke up early in the morning to prepare for my Bulawayo journey, Richard, Elizabeth and John went to see me off. When the bus arrived, I looked for an empty seat near the window. I preferred a vantage point not miss any view on the way. As the bus pulled off, I waved goodbye.

Like all country roads, the road was rough and bumpy, but that did not deter me from fantasising about the city. I thought of the high rising buildings I heard people talking about and my curiosity increased and as I thought of the delicious meals, my mouth watered.

After travelling for a long distance, I noticed the road was now smooth and when I looked, I realised we were now on a tarred road. Still perplexed by the tar, yet another development struck me. I noticed some isolated houses that appeared gorgeous.

"Tickets in your hands, please!" the conductor shouted.

We all searched our pockets or bags and handed him the tickets.

As the bus sped, I noticed an increase of traffic and

mushrooming of buildings and I presumed we had reached the city. My heart started beating faster when I thought what if Sophie did not turn up to meet me, but I quickly brushed aside that negative idea.

As the bus moved on, the volume of traffic continued to increase and the cars appeared to be in a rush. The exquisite buildings were all over and I could see a network of interlocking roads. In some cases, our bus slowed down due to traffic jam. Eventually, the bus indicated and went into the terminus.

Fortunately, when the bus came to a halt I spotted Sophie and my cousin, Jack waiting for me and I breathed a sigh of relief and felt at ease. I alighted to a tremendous welcome after which we then walked to Sophie's house that was not very far from the bus terminus. On the way, I admired the houses constructed in a different way from those in the village. They were brick walls and asbestos roofs.

"This is a beautiful place," I said as I beamed in exhilaration.

"There's yet more to please you. This is just the outskirts of the city," Sophie explained.

I convinced myself that if the periphery was so lovely then the city should be astounding. I patiently waited for a treat. I also saw streetlights and I queried how they operated. My sister explained everything.

We reached Sophie's house and it was a beautiful three-roomed house. Unlike our huts that were scattered, the house was one unit with subdivisions. The floors were concrete and shiny. I needed to use the toilet and I wondered where to go. I looked for a bush or pit latrine to no avail. To my surprise, my sister told me the toilet was within the house. She demonstrated how to use it and the flushing system amazed me. Initially I was so embarrassed to use it.

At night, they used electrical lights switched on by the touch of a button, a total contrast from the village where we used smelly paraffin lamps. The streetlights also went on and I wondered who had switched them on all at the same time. This just reminded me of Uncle Dengenyeka's stories about Johannesburg. I was completely inspired and I wished to be a permanent resident of this beautiful city.

During dinner, the meal was delicious, buttered bread, fresh meat and vegetables. The staple food was always prepared from white maize meal and not the lousy millet we ate in the village. We also did not eat in groups but each one had his own plate.

Sophie stayed with her husband, two daughters, a son and my cousin, Jack. Jack was the son to my aunt who lived with uncle Dengenyeka. The ages of Sophie's children were five, three and one. The eldest was Wamnyima, followed by Miriam and the last one Lister. Jack was a middle-aged man who was unemployed and spent most of his time drinking beer.

My sister's husband was a Zambian and he worked in a furniture factory. Although his wages were below average, he managed to sustain his family well.

Jack normally went out beer drinking and came home late at night very drunk. You could hear him coming by his unmelodious song, staggering, shuffling and smelling of traditional beer.

"Beer is in control of your life, Jack. It's high time you gathered yourself and search for employment," Sophie would advise Jack from time to time.

He never took those advices but continued with his heavy drinking. Jack came to the city ten years ago but never did anything fruitful apart from ruining himself. He never returned to the village to visit my aunt.

One day Sophie sent me to go and fetch Jack from a nearby

Beer Garden called Sidudla. When I entered that place, I was shocked to find so many people having booze at the same spot.

When I located Jack, he did not even recognise me because he was engrossed in a row. A certain man was threatening to assault him but he looked not bothered. The whole scenario made my heartbeat pound heavily.

"I'll kill you!" The man shouted while the crowd tried to restrain him.

"I'm going to buy a knife and I'll come back to slit your throat," the man threatened as he headed to the canteen that serviced the beer garden.

Immediately the man left, still fidgety, I forced myself among the crowd to reach for Jack. I tried to persuade my cousin to leave but he was so intoxicated that he could not listen to me. Frustrated, I left him, quickly squeezed myself among the multitude and followed that man to the canteen to see if he really wanted to buy the knife.

When I arrived, he had not yet bought it because there were too many customers. I kept on wishing if he could just give up the evil idea.

"May I have that knife," the man demanded pointing to an okapi, a popular knife used by thugs.

When he uttered those words, I felt breathless, fearing for my cousin's life. I hoped for the shopkeeper to do something that would save my cousin from the bloodthirsty monster.

"What do you want to do with it?" The shopkeeper asked because the mood of that man was dreadful.

I felt my breathing slowing down a bit hoping that question would be enough to put off the would-be murderer.

"Don't ask me questions! Stop wasting my time, I'm the one paying for it!" The man fumed at the shopkeeper.

"I'm not selling it to you, instead I'm calling the police," the shopkeeper insisted.

The shopkeeper's response relieved me more and I felt as if somebody had taken off from my shoulders a very heavy load. That fiend gave up and walked away. Thank goodness, he headed in a different direction and my cousin survived for another day.

I noticed that life here was not very friendly unlike in the village where people greeted each other and cared for one another. Even if you shared a seat in the bus, there was no conversation. I did not like that aspect of the city, it seemed strange to me.

Sophie and her husband also had booze but only on weekends. They were mild drinkers and did not behave like Jack. In most cases, they bought beer and drank in their house.

I had been in the city for a week but I had not yet travelled to the city centre. One morning Sophie took me there and we used a local bus. It did not take long to reach the city centre because it was not very far away. Had it not been for traffic jam and traffic lights I think we could have taken less time.

As soon as I alighted from the bus, the beauty of the place struck me. The buildings stood tall and some seemed to touch the sky and I wondered how they were constructed. Streets were long, wide and packed with various modes of vehicles. Beautiful and exotic trees lined the streets. There were also pedestrians who crossed the road at designated places. Every one seemed to move fast and that hustle and bustle confused me.

Some people would enter the shops while others would come out and the rest paced up and down the street. I came to appreciate that it was impossible to greet each and everyone otherwise; one would spend the whole day just greeting.

People were immaculately dressed, some in suites and others

in casual gear. I could hardly see anyone scruffy or dirty. I envied the way they looked. "This must be the place to stay in if I could successfully complete my schooling." I thought to myself.

We went into one store, a very large departmental store and I found that it was selling a big variety of items compared to the village store. The shops were self-service allowing customers to select what they wanted.

My sister bought me a new shirt, shorts and a pair of shoes. I was very delighted and thanked her for her generosity. Deep in me, I knew I would be the best at Nemane. After shopping, we went back to her house and that experience was wonderful.

"Did you see our town?" Wamnyima asked.

"It's a marvellous place." I said as I showed him the items my sister had bought me.

"Oh! They're wonderful." He said as he admired my shoes.

"Thanks."

I spent most of my time visiting recreational places like the nearby park which had amusing activities. I enjoyed boarding the mini train after paying a few cents. Its rounds were thrilling and fascinating as we could also see different scenery and terrains. The place was well cared for with beautiful flowers and lush green lawn.

Sometimes musical groups came to perform at the park by performing a variety of music and dance and I made it a point to take some skills to the village. There was also a cycling club where mentors taught children road signs and riding cycles. I found these lessons to be valuable as they groomed children to be good road users, hence minimise road accidents.

At night, we played out with my nieces and my nephew and sometimes my new friends joined us. I learnt new games to teach my friends in the village. They also asked me to teach them the games we played in the village, which they liked too.

We played on the streets that had streetlights. There was no danger of snakes and scorpions although sometimes the drunkards disturbed us on their way from Sidudla.

When time came to return to Nemane my heart sank, knowing all the enjoyment and comfort I had experienced would boil to zero. Wamnyima and my new friends were disappointed.

The following morning I left for Nemane and by midday, I had arrived. Richard, Elizabeth and John met me at the bus station. They were anxious to know about my trip and I did not disappoint them as I made great effort to narrate each encounter. They were grateful to receive the grocery Sophie had bought for the family. At school, I was the centre of attraction as other pupils were burning to hear about my visit.

The term continued well and in no time ended. I got the first position again at the end of my primary three. I made my way to Vulashaba after being away for eight months.

❖21❖
DISAPPOINTING NEWS

In Vulashaba, the whole family was happy to see me again. I knew they had a lot to share since I had not been home the previous school holiday. I also could not wait to tell them about the pulsating activities of Bulawayo city.

"Why did you not come home the previous school holidays? We missed you so much!" Langton said.

"I had gone to visit Sophie in Bulawayo."

The ones who had never been there became restless wanting to know about the place, luckily, it was my subject of interest.

"Is Bulawayo like Vulashaba?" Asked Lot one of our neighbours.

Before I could answer, I could not resist breaking into laughter. How could he compare a city to a remote village? Some Vulashaba folks did not even know Tsholotsho Business centre.

"Bulawayo is not a village but an urban area. The building structures are completely different from our huts." I tried to explain.

"How different do you mean?" Another local boy asked.

"The houses are made from bricks and roofed on asbestos, iron sheets or tiles. Their roads are not dusty like ours, but have tarmac that make them smooth."

To most that did not make sense, just Greek to their ears. I comforted them by saying, just like me their chance would come. Following that, we talked about the local issues. Tennyson related to me very sad news.

"Do you know that I've stopped attending school?" He said.

"Why is that so?" I asked in amazement.

"It's not only me. All the children stopped," Tennyson, elaborated.

"You're not serious," I said as I could not believe what I had just heard.

"The whole of last term we never went to school."

Realising the seriousness of the way he talked, I decided to listen to him. He then explained why they had stopped. The families they boarded with nearer to school had mistreated them and they all decided to discontinue school.

I was now the only child attending school. I could hardly believe they were all mistreated. How could it be when they were staying with different families? It could only be the bad influence of Vulashaba children, I thought. I could only see a gloomy future for them. They would either face permanent peasant life or put their lives on the line as they brave the hazardous obstacles of going to work in South Africa. Bulawayo had very little opportunities for people without educational qualifications.

I started to recall the day my father brought the heart-rending news that the school had no vacancy for me. I remembered pretty well, how I felt. I thought I was the most unfortunate but now the scenario was the opposite. If the school had accepted me, may be like my siblings I could have also dropped out. I realised now that it was a blessing.

Sometimes when decisions do not go our way we complain but when events unfold later, we start to appreciate the past. In spite of everyone of my family being out of school, I was determined to soldier on.

During my stay, I continued with the normal chores at home which included herding cattle and taking them to the cattle dip. I also played with the village children who continued to ask countless questions about Bulawayo.

The school holiday lasted for five weeks and time to go back to school drew closer. When the day to leave arrived, I faced a daunting challenge; it was the greatest decisive test to prove my determination to continue with school. The current rains had left the roads waterlogged making accessibility difficult. No bus could come closer to Vulashaba. The nearest connecting point was at Sipepa, 60km (37 miles) away and the only option would be to walk to that place. That was a mammoth task for a twelve year old. The journey involved travelling through thick forests often infested by wild animals. When moving across villages, I also risked confrontation by bullyboys. Because of the distance, the journey had to take some days. I made up mind to face the hurdle headlong.

The day I left for Nemane, I woke up at dawn. Mum wished me a safe journey and I started my long, lone trip with a small bag on my shoulders. As I passed through the thick forests, I thought of the lions and elephants and felt very nervous. I imagined if attacked by the lion, it would devour my whole body and probably nobody would ever discover my remains. Despite the challenging situation, I forged ahead praying for protection throughout. Any unfamiliar noise gave me a terrible feeling.

After about five kilometres of travelling in the bush, I reached the next village and I felt relieved. As I was sweating and thirsty I passed by a borehole to quench my thirst and I then proceeded on my journey. When I became hungry, I ate my small provision. When I had none left, I helped myself to edible wild fruits.

It was a gruesome journey but I persevered. At about sunset, I had already covered a reasonable distance, being exhausted I decided to put up at a certain homestead. The people who offered me a place to sleep encouraged me by saying I was not far from Sipepa.

In the morning, I resumed my travel. Fortunately, the children of that homestead attended the school on my way, so I had company.

I had anticipated that the journey would be easier since I had company but that was not to be. The waterlogged points on the road made walking even more taxing. Where there was no standing water they were wet clay soils that caused havoc by making the road slippery. We however plunged into those puddles and in some cases water rising above our knees. I became convinced that the bus had a valid reason not to come.

My accompaniment soon ended when those children branched to their school. They informed me that I had about 10km (6 miles) to cover. They advised me that some children from the village where I would catch the bus attended at their school. I decided to wait for them for company. While they were at school, I loitered at the local shops.

At 1pm, they finished school and I resumed my journey with those strangers. Their presence stimulated me as we journeyed along. Though the clay soils and puddles still wreaked havoc, we went on. We reached their village at sunset and their parents allowed me to spend that night in their homestead.

I was so fatigued, wrecked, that at bedtime, I slept throughout the night like a log. I only woke up at dawn when the father of the home knocked at the door advising his children to prepare for school. I also quickly prepared myself for the journey ahead.

After appreciating their hospitality, I left. They informed me I had about twenty kilometres (twelve miles) to cover and I wondered what the people in the village I slept first meant when they said I was close to Sipepa.

The journey ahead was to be a lone one and even so, I was still determined. Mile by mile, I continued with the count down. By midday, I reached Sipepa with a big relief! My muscles were aching, I had developed rash between my thighs due to pressure of walking and my lips were dry and cracking.

I reached there in the very nick of time and I made it into the bus. The bumpy road did not affect me negatively, but acted as a lullaby, as I slept all the way through to Tsholotsho. We were there by late afternoon.

Sadly, there were no buses covering the Nemane route, as the excessive rains had not spared those roads either. Since I felt rotten, I spent a night there. One of Richard's cousins, who owned one of the shops there, accommodated me.

The following day I started my journey to Nemane, which was twenty-three kilometres (fourteen miles) away. I felt the exhaustion and my feet were sore with blisters, however, I had no choice but to move on. My journey was a calm one as I met very few people on the way. I kept wondering if that peace would last. Still worried, moving in a bushy area, a very strange and harsh voice disturbed me.

"Hey, stop there if you don't want any trouble!" An older boy shouted as he approached me. "Handover all the cash you have," he said, showing me an open palm.

I knew he was a bully and that I was in hot soup. I gathered my courage and responded.

"I'm sorry, I've no money," I answered apologetically.

"You're kidding! I'm not here for jokes!" He said as he grabbed me by the collar and started searching all my pockets and my bag.

As he searched me, I became terrified and started shivering thinking he would discover my trick and therefore face repercussions of lying. I had hidden my bus fare in one of my socks, luckily, he never searched that far.

"Go, you pauper!" He shoved me and let go.

I made a few shaky steps and I heard him shouting again.

"Next time you must carry money, otherwise you will be punished!" The bully threatened again.

I quickly continued walking away as if nothing had happened. I never make an effort to look back just in case he changes his mind and calls me back. After walking for a distant and having taken a corner, I gathered the guts to check if I had escaped from that rowdy boy. I breathed a sigh of relief when I noticed he was nowhere near and thanked goodness that I had escaped unscathed.

I ran for about half a kilometre to clear from danger. Realising he was not in pursuit, I walked the rest of the distance. On my way, I was still wary of meeting another one.

I carried on and by sunset, I had reached Nemane. I was very happy to have survived an attack by a bully. Overall, I spent three nights on my way. The adverse effects of the long journey had begun to take toll; my whole body was aching with a feeling of extreme exhaustion. I doubted if I would fully recover again from that awful feeling.

"Welcome!" John said as he came to meet me.

"Thank you, John."

"You look worn out. What's the problem?" John quizzed.

"My friend, I had a very hard time. I walked most of my

journey here."

"Why?" John looked puzzled.

"There were no buses. The swampy roads made it impossible for them to move. Look at my feet. They are a testimony of what I went through," I said as I showed him my blistered feet.

"I'm sorry about that, pal. If I may ask, how's Tennyson doing?"

"He's fine."

We then walked to meet the rest of the family. They also welcomed me and asked how the Vulashaba family were keeping.

"Why are you coming so late? Don't you know schools opened two days ago?" Elizabeth asked.

"Travelling to this place was no child's play." I said as I also showed her my feet.

I related to her the hurdles that I overcame and she could not resist sympathizing with me. Tears filled her eyes. The rest of the family also felt sorry for me.

The following day I went to school and explained my ordeal to the teacher who also pitied me. Most of my classmates were happy to see me as they thought I had decided to stay in Vulashaba.

❖ 22 ❖
OUR SCHOOL TRIP

Time moved very fast and I found myself in primary six. During all school holidays, I had been making visits to Vulashaba. As the only child left schooling, one would have expected my whole family to back me up financially, but unfortunately, I continued to struggle. It appeared my parents had no insight for education and that was why they never bothered when my siblings decided to discontinue school.

My school organised a trip to Matopo Hills, a tourist resort area where they buried the famous Cecil John Rhodes. Zimbabwe's former name Rhodesia derived its name after him. The fee was only one dollar fifty cents (one pound fifty pence). Although a small amount now, those days it had value because it covered transport costs and provision.

About ninety pupils paid for the trip and John was among them. I really did not want to miss out but my sister Elizabeth told me she could not raise that amount.

"Robbie, have you paid for the trip?" I asked my friend at break time.

"You know my parents wouldn't afford. What about you?" Robbie asked.

"Not yet. I don't want to miss a trip of a lifetime," I answered.

"Hmm…you're as poor as I am?" Robbie scoffed.

"I've got a solution," I continued.

"What solution? Why not forget about it?"

"Our class teacher might help," I suggested.

"I doubt," he replied.

I then explained to him my plan. I would ask for a piece job and this would only work if Robbie were involved. As this excited Robbie, we approached the teacher together.

"Can we please talk to you about the coming trip?" I said as I introduced the subject.

"What about it. I'm not the one collecting the fares."

"We know that. We've a request," I added.

"What is it, boys?"

We offered to make her a vegetable garden and to continue nurturing it even after the trip. In return, she would pay for our trip. She agreed.

We had the job done in two days, but it was not a stroll in the park, as we had to cut logs and carry them on our shoulders one by one from about a kilometre away. Our teacher was so impressed that she rewarded us even more and we were exceedingly grateful for her generosity.

We were leaving very early in the morning for our trip to Matopo Hills and to avoid any delays, all pupils put up in school. That evening, we were wild with excitement, played games and ran around the school grounds and our teachers asked us to go to bed. They had prepared two classrooms for that purpose, one for the boys and the other for girls.

We slept packed like sardines but that did not bother us. We continued chatting in the classrooms and I do not know when we actually fell asleep. The next thing I heard were the voices of some teachers as they came to wake us up. We threw our blankets aside, wiped our faces and joined the girls in the bus. The atmosphere was just electric as we looked forward to the adventure ahead. Having all assembled in the bus, the journey to Matopo Hills started.

The thrill continued throughout the journey as we sang, whistled and chatted. We reached Bulawayo at sunrise and proceeded to Matopo hills after being told we would tour the city on our way back. We arrived at Matopo Hills at about 8 am and we alighted from the bus to have a full view of the place.

The view was stunning, chains of mountains stretched endlessly. The spectacular granite rocks were amazing and the scene of that exotic formation of granite boulders was unique. We climbed up the mountains and the experience was exhilarating. We explored the huge caves were Bushmen used to stay. They left a legend of their stone paintings, which have survived for centuries.

Matopo Hills is also a home for a well-stocked game park. We had the opportunity to see both large and small animals in their natural environment. We enjoyed seeing zebras galloping with herds of sables and antelopes close by. We also saw baboons carrying their babies on their backs while some were gathering wild fruits. It was a joy to see these animals feeding and drinking water at a close range.

The behaviour of the wild animals was different from those found in the village. The few animals we saw in the village galloped away as soon as they met us, maybe their instincts compelled them to do so because villagers hunted them.

That wildlife wonderland was not only rich in animals, but also infested with bird life. It boasted a large variety of birds never seen in our village. It was a pleasure to watch them, some at a very close range.

We had our lunch at a well spread rock where we had a beautiful view. Drinks and bread served was a great lunch for us because we hardly had such at our homes. We enjoyed our lunch so much that you could only hear lips smacking as children licked the sweetness of juice off their lips.

After lunch, we proceeded to a scene called Rhodes View which is the burial spot for Cecil John Rhodes and other prominent settlers. Because of their neat condition, we believed the graves were well cared. They looked like recent graves and the marble stones used still had their original sparkle.

We continued exploring the area enjoying its vegetation, which was very different from that of Nemane. We were tired because most of the time we were up the mountains and for most of us, it was our first time to climb mountains, as they were none in Nemane.

We left for Bulawayo late in the afternoon. We viewed the city centre and the city park. At that time, some pupils gathered around me and asked me about Bulawayo since I had visited there before. Skyscrapers, traffic lights and heavy traffic stunned most pupils. They wondered why cars stopped when lights were red and proceeded when they became green. The teachers explained that no one operated the lights but they were automatic and programmed.

We also had an opportunity to window-shop and do some shopping in big supermarkets. Most pupils did not know what to do in self-service stores and our teachers had a tough time trying to explain everything. With my pocket money, I bought a packet of fresh chips and I enjoyed them.

The teachers took us to public toilets and most pupils were

stunned more. Some were afraid to sit on toilet sits and even tried to escape when toilets flushed. Pupils also enjoyed drinking water from the taps.

Another thing that also astounded pupils was the huge population of people who moved up and down the pavements each one concerned with his business.

We also visited the National Museum, which we enjoyed so much. Here we were able to see a variety of stuffed animals, which were a replica of real lions, zebras and elephants. Some of these animals looked as if they were alive. We had the opportunity to learn a great deal about the history of our country. The museum is spherical shaped and we went up and down the stairs and to exit, we found ourselves at the other end, and we were astonished.

At dusk after we had toured Bulawayo, we left for Nemane. The frenzied atmosphere continued and we sang and danced all the way. When we arrived, we alighted from the bus and it made its way back to its garage in Bulawayo. Since we arrived late at night, we therefore put up at school. Due to exhaustion and fulfilment of all our anxious expectations, we retired without noise unlike the day before our tour. What great excitement and what an expedition!

John and I left for home very early in the morning and we looked forward to relating our life experiences to the family. We knew they would also be eager to know about the trip.

They welcomed us well and we shared with them so much about our tour. The following day it was school as usual and the main talk was about the trip.

⋘ 23 ⋙
MY FINAL YEAR IN PRIMARY SCHOOL (15 YEARS OLD)

My school received an award for being the best school in the district in academics, administration as well in sports. Among the prizes was a sizeable library books. With those books, the teachers decided to start a library within the school.

My school had no librarian and most teachers had already too many responsibilities so they chose me to act as a librarian. I was glad to carry out the task. I worked voluntarily during breaks and a few minutes after school finished. I issued out, received back the books, and kept the records of these transactions. Our library was equipped with a variety of books, fiction and non-fiction novels, and science and history books. Most books were in English and some in vernacular.

The privilege was of great benefit to me as it inspired me to be a bookworm. As I did not want the chore of herding cattle after school to deter me from reading, I devised a method to help me pursue my hobby. As the saying goes," Where there's a will, there's a way."

I managed to read a variety of novels whilst herding cattle and that helped me so much in developing English as my second language. Among the novels, I read, as a herd boy was 'Tom Sawyer' and 'Oliver Twist'. I divided my time between looking after cattle and reading a few pages until I finished the novel.

It went for a long time enjoying reading while herding cattle and everything seemed to move well. One day, as I became engrossed in the novel and hoping John kept vigilant, the cattle strayed. They went into a protected paddock reserved for winter grazing. There were people guarding that paddock and as we went in to drive the cattle out, they caught us red-handed. Before we could escape, I heard one of them shouting, "Stop those boys!"

Those words took us by surprise for we had thought we had managed to sneak out undetected. We knew we had to act fast to save ourselves.

I looked at John and he looked at me in non-verbal communication about the course of action to take. I contemplated taking their orders to stop but something compelled me not to. Other herd boys had been in hot soup for letting cattle stray into that paddock.

We never uttered words to each other but took to our heels. The men were in hot pursuit but could not cope with our speed. They unleashed their dogs on us out of desperation.

The dogs came charging fiercely at us, John surrendered, and dogs soon pounced on him. Some dogs headed straight at me and I realised it was a matter of time before they caught up with me, but despite that, I was resolute not to give up. To avoid dogs pouncing on me, I decided to con them. I pretended to be encouraging them to catch an animal. The dogs fell for my trick and quickly ran in front of me. The men never gave up but continued putting pressure on me.

To make matters worse, that place was open grassland and there was no bush to hide. Exhaustion finally caught up with me and I surrendered. Those men still panting and tempers flaring got hold of my arm and started manhandling me. I knew I was in for it especially after making them sweat for my capture.

"You think you're clever! You'll pay for this!" One of the men threatened as he grabbed me by the arm.

The men were just fuming, shouting and swearing. I did not answer back but stood in a frozen state, my heart beating faster due to exhaustion and fright. They frog marched me up to the point were they had apprehended John.

"That boy must be punished more severely than the other one! He made us run all that distance!" said one of the men pointing an accusing finger at me.

"That's true," concurred the other men.

"Strip them naked and let them lie on the ground face down," commanded their leader.

I knew we were in for a thorough beating especially that we defied their instructions to stop. With no other option, I had to brace my self for any eventuality.

They took turns to cane us and whipped us mercilessly and as they did so, I experienced an intense pain on my back. I remained defiant and never made any sound as I was prepared to suffer in silence. All of a sudden John bellowed like an ox struck by a spear.

"Please forgive me!" John screamed pleading for mercy.

They stopped caning him but intensified on me. As they did so, they continued uttering abusive words and saying, I deserved more as I made them run too much. Regardless of that, I remained tight lipped without a whine, and they only stopped whipping me at their own discretion and set us free.

We could not walk properly because of our bruised and sore bum but sadly, we still had had to drive the cattle back home. It was one of the most intense bashing, I ever experienced. It was tough to drive cattle and our home seemed to have been further than the usual distance. On the way back, we never talked about our mishap.

On arrival home, we shut the cattle in their kraal and went to report our ordeal to the elders. They did nothing about it except blame us on our lack of vigilance. My bottom was swollen and tender and I could hardly sleep that night. I was just spluttering with anger and the spirit of vengeance.

The following day was a school day and I went to school as if nothing happened. I could not even tell my friends because they would probable laugh at me. Sitting on the hard benches was an ordeal because of the unbearable pain.

The pain and swelling took a long time to resolve. For our bruised bottoms, we received no treatment; not even a painkiller. We healed up naturally and one would think I would have given up reading a novel while herding cattle. I never yielded, but did it with due care.

We had a school quiz on general knowledge including History and Geography and as one of the outstanding pupils; the school selected me to be the leader of that club. The teachers tasked me to set out some of the quiz questions. I loved that and it helped me improve my general knowledge.

My school responsibilities increased so did my confidence. Once when we the school celebrated the achievement of 'The Best Performance Award', they chose me to be a poet. It involved entertaining invited guests and the audience by displaying my dancing agility and speech eloquence. I also participated in the Shakespeare drama, "The Taming of the Shrew" taking a leading role in taming the shrew. The ceremony was big, as the school had invited other neighbouring schools. I vividly recall that big ceremony. All those activities occurred in my final year in primary school.

My brother Elias who lived in South Africa intended to marry. He had never met his in-laws and customarily, the in-laws could only release their daughter for marriage after they had seen their son-in law to be. Due to circumstances beyond his control, my brother could not come for the betrothal party. My family tasked me to represent him and equipped me with hints on how to pose as a son-in-law.

On that day, I dressed up like an adult and went to spend the night at my brother's wife-to-be's home, representing him. I conformed to all necessary norms as advised. It was successful because after that my brother's in-laws released their daughter. I think my acting skills helped me to perform to that level.

My seven years of primary education ended after writing the final exams. I had prepared well for them and I wrote in a relaxed mood. I only looked forward to progressing to secondary school.

I thanked the Gumbo family for the five years I spent with them. I had learnt and appreciated so much from that family. Among other aspects that I appreciated mostly, was their social and spiritual life. Due to the number of years I had stayed with them, it was not easy to part.

Finally, I had to rejoin my family for good and only return to collect my exam results.

❖ 24 ❖
WAITING FOR MY EXAM RESULTS

The sun was setting in its crimson cradle through the thick forests as I entered my Vulashaba home, but it provided adequate light though, that my family could not miss my lone figure as they ran to welcome me with multiple warm hugs. Mum used the opportunity to acknowledge the vital role played by my sister and her in-laws during my whole stay with them.

We had so much to discuss with my folk that evening. They enquired about my exams and I reassured them that I was hopeful. I also requested for an update with the goings in Vulashaba.

I heard about a chilling incident that occurred during my absence. It took place at the same route I used the year I walked to Nemane.

One a clear night, full moon beaming onto the thick forest, my Mum and her friends had a very nasty experience as they returned from a beer drink in a happy mood. They were twelve of them, walking in a single file in a narrow path. Beside the path, in front of them, they noticed a gigantic figure and as they were under the influence of alcohol, they just forged ahead.

Suddenly the huge beast flapped its ears and a deafening trumpet followed. Nobody told anyone what to do; they scrambled and scurried to seek refuge as they realised that it was an elephant. Due to fright, everyone became sober and they raced back to the village they were coming from.

In a state of panic, the group broke up into small numbers. On arrival, at the home, they just pushed their way into the huts, as they did not want the elephant to catch up with them in case it decided to be on hot pursuit. The home occupants were surprised with the arrival of the first group who panted and some had panic attacks. Obviously, they had to spend the night there.

I shrugged as they finished narrating the story as I imagined if the elephant had trampled my Mum to death. A cold chill ran down my spine.

The following day Dad sought to have a conversation with me. I suspected I must have wronged him, as it was not his norm to have a dialogue with us as his children.

"I've decided to exempt Tennyson and you from herding cattle. Your younger brothers will take over."

I was grateful for that great news and when I relayed the news to Tennyson, he was thrilled too. He celebrated by punching the air with his fist. Easy holiday I had, visiting friends and a bit of mischief.

My half-brother, Pedias, who worked in South Africa, came home and we were happy to see him. He told us many good things about South Africa and also informed us that Elias, Jabulani, Edmond and Nelson were all fine. He had brought us assortments of gifts and my family had a happy festive season.

The schools were about to reopen for the New Year [African

school year runs from January to December] and I looked forward to starting my secondary school education, however none of parents spoke about my further education or let alone collecting my results. That got me worried as I thought there was no more further education for me.

With my schooling being uncertain, I approached my Mum who told me she could not afford secondary education fees. She could only give me the little she had hoping my sister Sophie would top up. I could see my dream shuttered and seven years spent in primary school a complete waste. I never bothered asking my Dad because since we moved to Vulashaba, he had relinquished his duties of paying our fees. In Nemane, he had paid them from the little carpentry earnings, but he had given up the trade.

With meagre resources, I decided on attending a day school in Bulawayo rather than a boarding school that was expensive. I just hoped things would work out.

With decisions made, I was to leave for Nemane to collect my exam results, but once again, the journey would be tough because of the waterlogged roads. The rains were one of the heaviest I had ever seen. This time, I would have to walk even a longer distance as all buses from Bulawayo could only go as far as Tsholotsho Business Centre, the only road with tarmac. To reach Tsholotsho, I would have to walk one hundred kilometres (sixty-two miles) and from Tsholotsho, I would walk a further twenty-three kilometres (fourteen miles) to Nemane. I was prepared to do anything just to get through with my education.

Luckily, this time around I would not have to travel alone, Pedias was also due to return to Johannesburg. He was to catch a bus for Bulawayo in Tsholotsho. I was almost sixteen and I hoped I would cope well than when I was only twelve. The day before I left, Mum gave me some money she had reserved after selling an ox.

At sunrise, we bid the family farewell and left for our journey. To remain on the right track, we decided to follow the bus route, though in some places, the route was bound to meander. We forged ahead through the sands of the forest.

As we walked, Pedias told me stories about Johannesburg, which reminded me of my late uncle Denyenyeka and I could visualise him sitting around the bonfire relating his experiences. That kept us occupied and diverted our minds from the stress of walking.

By midday, we had covered a reasonable distance and signs of exhaustion were apparent. The active conversation had died out and the only sound heard was the thumping of our feet.

As we approached the corner of the road, we noticed a small shop and Pedias suggested we stop for refreshments. With renewed vigour, we proceeded on our journey.

When it got too dark, we asked for accommodation at one homestead close to the road and they welcomed us and offered us a free room for the night. They also provided us with food for supper. I slept like a log until Pedias woke me up early morning so we could continue our journey.

We had no further stopover on the way, and by two in the afternoon, we were at Tsholotsho. My brother continued his journey by bus to Bulawayo and I put up at Tsholotsho with my cousin, Jack who had improved on his drinking. He had left Bulawayo for Tsholotsho where he worked in a farm.

I proceeded to Nemane alone the following morning. Even though I was still tired but not as haggard as I had been the day before, I was determined to complete my journey. My wish was not to meet any bully who would complicate my already stressful journey.

Thank God, it was not one of those hot summer days common

in Africa. [The African summer, the rainy season, is November to April.] Second by second, minute by minute and hour by hour, I was nearing my destination. It was a lousy and uneventful journey.

I arrived at Nemane late in the afternoon and I could not proceed to school because it was after hours. Even if the school was open, I do not think I would have managed to seek for the head teacher because I was not myself, both physically and mentally and wanted nothing else except to have a good rest.

After my sister and everyone else had welcomed me, I did not even have time for food or a bath. I told them of my intention to go to bed straightaway and with their blessing, I retired for the night. I do not remember turning and tossing, but was only awakened in the morning by the ever-shining African sun which threw its rays through the cracks of the old door of our hut.

I then quickly prepared myself and made my way to school. On arrival, the headmaster's door was open. I knew that he was in although it was still school holidays.

"Why are you coming so late? The results were out three weeks ago and most secondary schools have done their selection," commented the headmaster. After a breather, he continued, "Anyway, congratulations you made it, your results are outstanding," he shook my hand as he said that.

I looked at the results as well and I was very pleased. After thanking the headmaster, I quickly dashed home to show my sister and her family. They were impressed.

The following day I walked to Tsholotsho to get a bus to Bulawayo. I did not want to cause any further delay in my mission to enrol at secondary school.

❖❖ 25 ❖❖
I START SECONDARY SCHOOL (16 YEARS OLD)

When I arrived in Bulawayo, I went to stay temporarily with Richard's elder brother and his family as Sophie and her children were out of town. I had met the family before when they visited their parents in Nemane. As I arrived late, I could not proceed to schools to look for a secondary school place, but deferred everything to the following morning. As people here told me that, most secondary schools had completed their enrolment, I wondered if I would get a vacancy.

In the morning, they assigned a girl to take me to a particular school and from the little information I had, it was not a prestigious school as it catered for pupils who did not do well in primary. It specialised only in technical subjects such as metalwork and woodwork, which was not my interest.

As I wanted to pursue academic subjects, I told the girl to take me to Mpopoma High School which had a very good academic reputation and she agreed. When we arrived there, the clerk had this to say, "I'm really impressed with such good results from a rural school. Why did you delay? Our enrolment is now full," the clerk commented.

His initial comment made me very hopeful, but as he progressed, it was as if he had pierced my heart with a spear. Still feeling the pain, I saw him pick the phone and rung Mzilikazi High School. Mzilikazi ordered me to hurry as they had only two vacancies left. I thanked him for his kind gesture and hurried to Mzilikazi.

We had walked about one hour to get to Mpopoma. As we had no bus fare, we walked to Mzilikazi and we took about thirty minutes. The clerk there welcomed me and echoed the same sentiments as the Mpopoma one and happily he enrolled me.

I liked the school because unlike Mpopoma, it offered advanced levels. Mpopoma pupils who successfully completed their ordinary level joined Mzilikazi. I managed to settle my $7, 70 fees for the first term with the money Mum gave me. I had nothing left to buy the uniforms.

After Sophie returned from her visit, I joined her family. She was now a single woman as her husband had returned to Zambia, his country of origin. He was redundant after the furniture shop he worked for retrenched most workers. Having lost the hope of finding an alternative employment, he left with their son, Wamnyima. My sister who was reluctant to migrate to a foreign country remained behind with their two daughters, Miriam who was eight and Lister, six. The city council had relocated her to a one-roomed accommodation. The room was in a block of four which meant a total of four families occupied each block. Each room was multipurpose, utilised as a kitchen, bedroom, dining and lounge.

The accommodation was located in Mabutweni, a suburb reserved for less privileged people. The four families shared a single toilet, which also functioned as a bathroom; consequently, this over used facility was always in a messy state. Since the toilet was located outside the houses, we feared using it at night just in case a thug pounced on us. There were no adequate streetlights and crime was rampant too. At night, the suburb was a no-go area and it was common particularly at weekends to find one or two human corpses resulting from brutal murder. Because of the squalid conditions, most people despised the residents of that area.

Though unemployed and receiving no benefits, Sophie managed to look for money to buy my uniform. She used to sell her hand-knitted jerseys which sometimes took her a whole month to finish just one. Life was difficult for her and the children, as she had to pay utilities, buy food and so on and with my coming burdens were exacerbated.

My new school was seven kilometres (four miles) away. I used a bus back and forth and my sister struggled with my bus-fare and lunch money. I spent the whole day at school and survived with a meagre lunch consisting of half pint milk and a plain half a loaf of bread.

Njabuliso became my first friend. Though taller and heavily built than me, we clicked very well. He was mature and of cool temperament and that character blended well with mine. We were both from rural areas and our backgrounds were similar. Some pupils despised us despite being older than most of them and they attempted to bully us but Njabuliso had to thwart their unbecoming moves.

"Wake up you village boys! This is Bulawayo City!" The bullyboy mocked us as he poked Njabuliso's head with his finger.

Little did he know he would not get away with his comic antics? My friend raged and there was no verbal communication between us. Suddenly Njabuliso stood up and came face to face with that boy. The boy froze with fear as the reaction had taken him by surprise. With dazzling power, Njabuliso smacked the boy on the left cheek and for a few moments, the boy stood dazed with no words to say.

"Why are you beating me? What have I done to you? I'll report you to the headmaster!" The shamed boy cried, as he walked away.

This had gone down well with me. The boy was even more embarrassed because his friends also ridiculed him. He never reported anywhere knowing he started the fiasco. That day and henceforth, the rest of the bullies respected us.

As days went by, we made more friends including Native and Shapestone. Shapestone was rather a cool character, but Native was naughty and sarcastic, but personally had no problem with that.

With time, cliques developed within the group. Native's naughty personality clashed with Njabuliso's cool character, fortunately Shapestone and I managed to keep the opposing forces at bay.

We spent most of our time exploring the city life and we were soon deeply interested in current affairs. We took turns to buy the local daily paper and enjoyed reading it. My friends' study patterns were different from mine and as a result, we never had any studies together.

Unlike in primary school, the competition was very stiff, as the school had selected pupils with good passes. I braced myself for it and in no time, I emerged to be the best student in History. I enhanced my studies by joining study groups at weekends.

I struggled with my fees as it appeared my parents had surrendered all the responsibilities to my sister, Sophie, who was unemployed. Every end of term I kept guessing if I would return to school and it was by God's grace that I completed my first year in secondary school.

Sophie compounded her problems by allowing too many relatives to stay with her. There was congestion in that one room, with sometimes about fifteen of us all sleeping and eating there. These women were old enough to fend for themselves, but all they did was to spend their time guzzling beer. Whenever Sophie had no money, those women never contributed to buy food but rather bought soft drinks and snacks which they never offered to anyone. We would just watch them eat.

My sister sacrificed the care of her children by increasing her drinking habits. I found myself having to take care of Lister and Miriam, preparing their meals, washing and ironing their clothes. Nobody pushed me into that, but circumstances did.

Despite the financial problems that beset me, I still managed to cherish my school days and enjoyed the company of my school friends. We always encouraged each other to think big to succeed in life. We helped each other to wean from the village to the robust city life. We might have had differences at times but never did they turn nasty.

A good number of my age mates who lived in Mabutweni left school prematurely to work in the city shops and industries. Some of them were my acquaintances though not very close. They had opted out for monetary gain and with their earnings; they dressed on the latest fashions, a sign that they were town boys. A poor boy like me could not match their expensive style. Even though I envied them, I told myself to stay focused in my education as somehow I had a feeling their decision had no long-term benefits. I also followed the wise advice my teachers used to give on the importance of education.

During my second year, my problems escalated and I had to apprise the principal of the school who sympathised with me. My principal was Mr Darwin and he was from England. By that time, my Dad had married his fifth wife who was one or two years younger than I was. My lowly background touched Mr Darwin and he decided to exempt me from paying school fees and also offered to cater for my uniforms. Oh what a relief!

Due to the never-ending financial problems, in her one room accommodation, my sister started running a shebeen (an illicit bar where alcohol in sold without a licence). On Friday and Saturday, it operated from 7pm until early morning hours and on Sunday, from 7pm to 10pm.

I was the bouncer serving beer to the patrons and it was my responsibility to maintain peace and order within the room. I reprimanded any patron who attempted to cause discord. The task was difficult and risky since I was still very young. The elderly patrons could harm me especially when intoxicated. If the need be, I hoped the other regular patrons would come to my rescue. I never enjoyed this task, but I had to help my sister bring food onto the table and I also needed pocket money for my bus fare and lunch.

Since I had busy weekend nights, I had to sleep during the day and that effectively took away my weekend study. It was also impossible to study on weekday evenings. After coming from a drinking spree, the relatives who stayed with us were not helpful. They will demand me to switch off the light as it hurt their eyes.

I had no choice but to quit my evening studies. Luckily, though, one local schoolteacher offered his classroom to some boys and me for use after school. Even during the holidays, we used this facility.

As the shebeen operated by my sister was illegal, it was a target for the police who wanted to stamp out crime within the area. The prohibited beer outlets were usually a safe-haven for criminals. The high volume stereo music became a menace to the neighbours.

When drunk, the patrons would sometimes fight each other and at times these fights spilled outside our house and the police got involved. Many times the police raided the shebeens and usually confiscated beer, and flog the patrons.

I vividly recall one Sunday night when the police landed on us, started putting everything in room upside down, as they did their search, promising to lockup everyone. I became petrified as I could see myself missing school the next morning. Gladly, they left with my sister and all the patrons, leaving me behind. On the way, they reprimanded and released them. Most of them chickened-out to the comfort of their bedrooms and the wilful ones moved to another drinking spot.

The situation here was not conducive to learning and I did not perform to my fullest capacity mainly because of that unfavourable environment. Somehow, I managed not to drink or smoke despite so much exposure to alcohol. I tried to strike the balance between schoolwork and selling beer.

At the end of my fourth year, I was supposed to write the Cambridge Ordinary Levels exams and the school, which assisted me with fees, did not cover examination fees as this money needed to be in British pounds. The £69, 00 fees was for the Cambridge University in UK who set and marked our exams. Since Sophie could not afford the required amount, the principal advised her to seek assistance from social welfare.

We went together to their offices and they flatly refused to assist. That was my last hope. Their decision severely devastated me and almost brought me to tears and I felt the four years of secondary education would go down the drain.

My sister looked at my gloomy face and could not help her tears rolling down her face. The officer was touched and had compassion on us and he finally agreed to pay the required fee. We thanked the officer for the assistance and deep in me I knew writing my ordinary levels and passing them would improve my life.

❖❖ 26 ❖❖
REFLECTING ON MY PAST

I passed my ordinary levels fairly well and with those qualifications, my life looked brighter. Opportunities for white-collar jobs offered by my country at that time required people with the qualifications I had attained.

I could foresee that the days I had 'bucket milk' as relish were over. Throughout my childhood, my family struggled for its needs. The certificate I had gained would be a channel for a better job enabling me to provide adequately for my family and myself. I knew that the soft drinks and tea I yearned for would now be readily available.

My fantasy about staying in a city was now a reality. I had escaped dark nights, dusty grounds and dull days associated with village life. The hustle and bustle of the city was now set to be my life. Dressing in 'ibhetshu', and crying for a stolen pair of shoes would now be history.

I would not herd cattle or wake up at 2am to till the unfertile soils anymore and my survival would no longer be dependent on an erratic Tsholotsho rainfall pattern. A brighter and promising future as a professional person now lay ahead of me. I would not sleep in a hut, on a hard floor, but in a house with a comfortable bed.

Looking back at my childhood, I could see all the obstacles and challenges that I went through. I came from a less-privileged family that never knew the importance of education, sad to say that among my family and relatives, none had reached secondary school.

I started school at nine and completed my O levels at twenty and by then most of my age mates had been working for years and that could have derailed me. My brothers could have also influenced me to go and work in South Africa but thank goodness, that did not happen.

I came from a complex family of twenty-three children and my father had five wives. Completing secondary education was just a miracle in itself.

One of my most critical experiences was when all my siblings dropped out of school and I never wavered, but decided to continue. Where did I get the courage and will power to keep going?

On two occasions, there was no transport to take me from Vulashaba to my school in Nemane and the only way to reach Nemane was to walk a distance of more than a one hundred and twenty three kilometres (seventy-five miles). Apart from the distance, the journey had its obstacles. I could come across dangerous wild animals while walking through the forests. Bullyboys were also a menace, during the process of trying to rob me; they could have murdered or maimed me.

My primary school was ill equipped and lacked facilities conducive to good education and when I started there, it had no library, an integral component for sound and good education.

Staying with my sister Elizabeth was a blessing because I learnt the advantages of monogamy. The Gumbo family, with a father who was a monogamist led a better life than we did. I learnt the influence of religion in moral development of the family.

The importance of good leadership in educational institutions should never be underestimated. Had it not been for the generosity and sensitivity of Mr Darwin, my secondary school headmaster, I could not have completed my secondary education. Lack of financial backing could have destroyed all my aspirations, leaving me with the dreaded prospect of becoming a permanent peasant farmer.

When I also look back at my life in a shebeen, there is nothing positive I gained, but I praise my God for His protection. I could have become wayward or an alcoholic.

❖ 27 ❖
I ENTER THE JOB MARKET {21 years old}

In 1980, my country had just regained independence from Britain and every primary school child was entitled to free education and as a result, school enrolments doubled and the influx of children created a shortage of teachers. The government enacted a policy to employ anyone with junior certificate and above as temporary teachers.

The teaching vacancies left were in rural schools which did not deter me as I gladly grabbed the opportunity to become a temporary teacher. I knew that would surely be my gateway to training.

With a salary, my life began to improve and things got better for my parents as well and they started realising the importance of education. Even the Vulashaba folks could notice some positive changes.

During my teaching stint, I enjoyed sports and my favourite sports were soccer and athletics. I was involved in training the teams and they did so well in soccer and athletics.

During my second year in my teaching post, I became traditionally married to a woman who had been my classmate during secondary school. She was also a temporary teacher by then. We did not formalise our marriage because we did not have sufficient funds for a white wedding. We deferred the white wedding to the future.

Three years on, I received an offer of a nurse-training course which excited me very much since it had been my wish to pursue a career in medicine. Nursing at least would be next to my desire to care for patients.

My training school was United Bulawayo Hospitals. I did not experience any financially problems because I had a monthly salary during training and actually, my salary quadrupled to what I earned as a temporary teacher.

Three months into my training, I met one patient in a medical ward who liked me. After learning that I stayed far from the hospital, he offered me his flat in town that he was about to vacate. He had bought a house in an exclusive suburb and the estate agent he rented the flat from gave him the prerogative to look for an alternative tenant. The offer was just too good to refuse.

I broke the wonderful news to my wife who could not believe how lucky we were. We then moved to the flat which was exquisite accommodation of our dreams.

Though my wife came from a monogamist family, she had a similar background as mine. Her father now a widower was struggling to look after his children. We helped him by allowing two of my wife's younger brothers to stay with us. We also decided to alleviate Sophie's problems by bringing, Lister her younger daughter to our family and it was also a way of thanking Sophie for assisting me with my education.

We were to be responsible for the total upbringing of the three children. We knew it was a tough task, but we were determined to carry it. My wife spent most of her time at her work place as she worked out of the city. She only came during the weekends and school holidays; occasionally I visited her whenever I had time-off.

Life was very comfortable in the flat. Just imagine a village boy staying in the heart of the city. The place was very convenient in many ways as we managed to do late night shopping and went to cinemas.

I still remember one incident that occurred when we visited one of the drive-in cinemas when we were in the company of a couple that drove us there. The drive-in cinema was jam packed with all model of cars. A very popular movie was on show and a big crowd had come to watch it. As the occupants of each car were couples, the atmosphere around was that of close intimacy, lovers coming to show how they cared for one another.

The movie was a thriller and it continuously tickled our spirits and we could not avoid keeping our eyes constantly glued on the big screen. Suddenly, the unexpected happened. The picture disappeared from the screen and there was dead silence. We were all disappointed thinking a technical fault had developed. As I thought, "What next?" a voice sounded through the public address system?

"Everybody, please listen to this important announcement. A knife wielding man is by our entrance seeking for a man who stole his wife to the cinema."

We all listened attentively to that strange message coming from a cinema sound system. For a moment, the broadcast left us perturbed. The four of us in the car looked at each other and during the process never uttered a single word.

"So, ladies and gentlemen as we don't want any commotion, the man and woman concerned should vacate our premises immediately."

What followed was rather a bizarre scene. We could hear terrible sounds of screeching brakes and screaming tyres as motorist scrambled to drive out of the place. Cars raced roughly, as the drivers attempted to drive at top speed, but luckily, no accident resulted from that crazy moment.

Within a few minutes, the place was almost empty with three quarters of the cars having left. I cast my eyes around to check for the knife-wielding man and he was nowhere. I do not know whether he gave up when he saw a man driving out with his wife during the pandemonium.

The big question that came to many of us was why the cars left in such a hurry: Is it because they wanted to avoid seeing a man fatal stabbing his rival? Were all of them in the company of other men's wives? If the former were the reason, then one would understand. However, if the latter prevailed, then my country had a serious problem. How could such a big number of men go out with other men's wives?

After the confusion subsided, the gripping movie resumed. I was very happy to see it to the end. The weird incident we witnessed was the talk of the town for a long time.

✥ 28 ✥
OUR WHITE WEDDING {27 years old}

Eventually, my three-year training came to a successful end and I qualified as a Registered Nurse. I did not have to struggle to look for employment, as it was the government's responsibility to deploy us. They allocated me to a rural hospital not far from my wife's work place, and I did not mind going to work there.

The hospital was in a growth point earmarked for a town and as a result, its facilities were up to standard. The staff accommodation was modern houses with electricity and piped water.

Antelope District hospital serviced all the surrounding villages, an area with a radius of roughly seventy kilometres (forty-three miles). Under it were nine satellite clinics and one mission hospital that referred to us the patients they were unable to manage.

The hospital had one hundred and ten beds. It had General Male and Female Wards, Paediatric, Infectious Disease, Maternity, Outpatient and Emergency Departments. Apart from the general hospital duties, we were involved in giving health education programme to the surrounding communities.

I enjoyed working in that hospital as I managed to gain immense experience. One of the doctors I worked with was Dr Ider, a very experienced doctor from Germany. She was always ready to teach us and as a result, I owe her a lot of gratitude for the knowledge she imparted to me.

We never rented out our flat when I worked out of Bulawayo, my two brothers-in-law and my niece remained there. Staying with these three youngsters was a pleasure and it was gratifying to see them grow and become independent and successful adults.

Two years after I qualified as a nurse, we decided to hold our white wedding which had been our dream for years. We wanted to make the wedding day lavish to imprint it in our minds for years. Since it would be the first white wedding in both families, we worked hard to close all loopholes that would have brought uncalled criticisms.

We chose the Bulawayo large City Hall as the venue for our wedding reception and since the venue was prestigious and sought-after place, we booked it in five months advance. We also booked the Small City Hall for dining purposes. We worked tirelessly towards the success of this day, as we knew none of our family members would be in a position to chip in with funds.

On that same year, we accepted Christ and we were baptised into the Seventh Day Adventist Church as we wanted to have a holy matrimony and proceed with celebrations afterwards.

Two months before the wedding day, a dark cloud hung over us. The estate agent who rented the flat to us decided to sell his block of flats giving the long serving tenants the option to buy first. This was a dilemma as buying the flat meant having to cancel the wedding and if we did not buy, the only option would be to move to the western suburbs, a place where we resided before moving into the city centre. Living there would not be as comfortable as in the flat.

While I preferred to proceed with the wedding preparations, my wife wanted us to defer it and buy the flat. After a lengthy discussion, we finally agreed to go ahead with our wedding preparations.

A month before the wedding, we had to vacate the flat and rented a house in the high-density suburbs. Life was not very comfortable there, but we told ourselves it would not be for long.

Meanwhile the wedding preparation continued. Our aspirations were so high and one of them was to capture our wedding in a video cassette. At that time, most people never knew about videos and it seemed like an impossible goal to achieve. It was only for the elite class. Somebody overheard one of the organisers of our wedding saying, "These people are crazy! How can they dream of a video recording when they don't even own a video player?"

Everything was now set for Sunday, our big day. Saturday morning looked lovely with a very clear sky, reassuring us that the weather would be favourable for the wedding. As the day progressed, everything changed, dark clouds hung from the sky signifying a very heavy downpour. That was not good news for us.

In the evening, it started pouring and it continued the whole night and I learnt the following day that my wife cried thinking the rain would adversely affect our wedding. For about three years, the whole country had experienced the worst drought in living memory and the dam levels had fallen dangerously low. Most cities, including the one I lived in, had introduced drastic water rationing by pronouncing a blanket ban on use of hosepipes. The lush green lawns and gardens that characterised the city had turned brown and some became non-existent.

The heavy rains continued to pound even on the morning of the wedding day leaving everybody puzzled of how things would proceed concerning transport to church and reception venue. I recall my Mum approaching me saying, "Son is this rain going to stop?" Before I could respond, she continued, "Will the wedding proceedings go ahead?"

"The Creator is the one who knows and if it is His will, everything will go as planned," I assured my Mum.

When the rains seemed not to stop, we decided to forge ahead and proceeded to the church as we were already an hour behind schedule. To make matters worse, I did not know what efforts my wife and her entourage were making as then they were no mobile phones and the houses where we were had no landlines. I just hoped for the best.

The rain was so heavy that even the city's drainage system could not cope. Bulawayo streets had become small rivers. Some cars broke down due to high levels of water and others wriggled through. In my lifetime, I have never seen such a heavy downpour.

As if we had communicated, my wife entourage also arrived at church the same time as ours. The pastor was already waiting. The service commenced but the rain continued pouring. During the forty-five minutes marriage ceremony, the pastor also made a comment on the downpour and comforted us by saying we should not worry, as rain is a blessing from God.

To conclude the ceremony, we had a prayer and before we closed our eyes for prayer, I had to take a quick glance at the situation outside and sadly I noticed that the rain persisted. The pastor prayed and immediately after, I looked outside again. Unbelievable-the rain had miraculously stopped and I breathed a big sigh of relief.

The wedding party proceeded to the city park for photographs.

People who had been decorating the wedding reception area joined us there too for photographs and my sister-in-law, Belina was among them and I secretly approached her to find out if there were guests in the hall as I was worried stiff the rains had scared them away. She assured me that quite a good number had already turned up and people continued trickling in.

I could hardly believe her as I thought she was just calming me down to keep me focused on the day. I continued thinking the wedding would be a flop, as only a handful of guests would attend. We stayed at the park for about an hour and then left for the small city hall.

The bridal team took about an hour having our dinner and after that, we marched into the large city hall and as we entered, I looked around and I was very happy to see the hall packed to capacity. My folks and friends had defied the heavy rain and turned up in numbers and the atmosphere was electric.

My Dad was there. As my grandfather, had eight wives and my great-grandfather had twenty-five, many of my Dad's half-brothers, sisters and cousins attended. My wife's relations did not disappoint too. The guests were about a thousand in total.

I felt like a king with such a huge crowd having come to grace my wedding day. I also looked at my dear wife and her dazzling beauty beamed like a ray of light. Everything went according to plan making the day a memorable one in my life.

At sunset, it was time to end the wedding celebrations and I clearly remember some of the words said by my uncle, Richard who gave the vote of thanks. He said that the heavy rains were a sign that the home of the newly weds would be characterised by 'bumper harvests'.

The following day all newspapers reported about the torrential rains that had broken more than one hundred years' record. All dams that had been critically below level were spilling over. Although the rains nearly spoiled our wedding day, they were most welcome because that spelt the end of the devastating drought experienced by our country.

❖❖ 29 ❖❖
THE FUTURE CONTINUES TO LOOK BRIGHTER

After the wedding, we gave ourselves a year to stabilise financially as the wedding had exhausted all our savings. When our finances improved, we set ourselves yet another goal. We bought a one-acre plot in a low-density suburb to develop our residential house. We sourced a mortgage from the bank to boost our savings and within a year, the house was ready for occupation. We started having a very comfortable accommodation again, only this time, the house was ours.

That same year, I embarked on my diploma in midwifery that would enhance my chances of promotion. I went to train at Mpilo Central Hospital in Bulawayo and on completion, I returned to my station. During that same period, my wife started her teacher-training course and that marked the beginning of a brighter future for us.

A few months after, the authorities appointed me the acting-nurse-in-charge of Antelope District Hospital. I was the overall in charge of nursing duties. It was a prestigious post for me as a mere village boy who had the first pair of shoes at the age of nine. I had never dreamt of that and I braced myself for that challenge. I co-ordinated patient care and it was my duty as well to stimulate the morale of the staff to increase their output.

Overall, I worked in that hospital for seven years and although I enjoyed my job, I had a desire to explore the profession in other countries and gain international exposure. The country that first came into my mind was South Africa, the land of plenty as my uncle Dengenyeka used to put it.

Unlike my other siblings who immigrated to that country illegally, I had no fear of crossing the crocodile-infested Limpopo River. I neither dreaded walking through the dangerous game park nor shuddered at meeting the South African police as I had acquired the necessary travelling documents before hand.

Before I made a move to South Africa, I decided to transfer to United Bulawayo Hospitals in Bulawayo where I did my general nursing. I wanted to make it easy to reorganise my family issues before I moved as it was difficult doing that from the rural areas. I was going to work as an ordinary nurse, a move that surprised some people. That did not bother me since I knew I was only there for a short period.

The management deployed me to the Accident and Emergency Department which initially, I did not like as I had hoped to work in Maternity. Since qualifying as a midwife, I had developed a keen interest in midwifery.

Their department was very big, busy and challenging and I prepared myself to meet the challenges headlong. As days went by, I gradually developed an interest in the department. What I liked was that, like in Maternity Department most of the work was not routine. We had to prepare for anything from severe trauma to minor ailment.

After almost a year in that hospital, I decided to make serious plans about my moving to South Africa. I then organised transport to take me there and Willie, one of my cousins who worked there offered me a lift.

We departed very early in the morning and by eleven o'clock, we were at the Beit Bridge border post. After going through immigrations formalities in both borders, we proceeded with our journey. As we went deeper, it was glaring evident that development in South Africa was more than in Zimbabwe. I saw complicated motorways with heavy traffic.

By 5pm, we had reached Johannesburg and the high-rise buildings I saw impressed me and that were the taste of what my uncle described to me when I was a small boy. The city had skyscrapers I had never seen before. My cousin drove me straight to my brother-in-law's flat, which was located within the city centre.

After the welcome, Poland offered me a cold drink and snack. Following that, he took me around his flat. We then discussed my itinerary. Poland gave me a newspaper, which advertised many vacant nursing posts and I made some applications and with my immerse experience, I never doubted getting one.

Before he took me around the hospitals, Poland decided to take me around Johannesburg, to experience the beauty of the place. Indeed, I could not stop gazing at its magnificent buildings.

The city had a fast pace and it surely looked like a shopping paradise – a place where one could purchase anything or everything. The shops ranged from top departmental stores to thriving flea markets. Poland informed me some shops opened until late at night and others operated round the clock.

After a day's tour of the city, we decided to go back to his flat and by then I felt very tired and I only recovered after taking some refreshments and a nap.

The following day we went to various hospitals and submitted my applications. During my one-month stay, I had so many offers and I simply needed to return to Zimbabwe and resign from my job formally.

However, the social life in that country never impressed me. The city was characterised by violence, which it did not manage very well. On two occasions during my visit, I came across thugs moving around with guns and that caused chills of fear down my spine. The daily papers and the local television showed frightening scenes of people killed in taxi wars and bank robberies.

The violence I saw made me doubtful about taking any job offer in that country. I returned home and thought of venturing into another country.

I decided to try Botswana because at that time the country had shortage of nurses. It was also doing well economically, politically and socially, although in terms of development, it was lagging behind South Africa and my country.

I made my application to the ministry of health in Botswana and within a short space of time; I received a positive response inviting me for an interview. I attended the interview and I became successful and after that, I returned to my country to serve two months notice.

I prepared to relocate to work in a foreign country and although, I anticipated problems of settling that did not discourage me as I was fascinated by new move.

❖❖ 30 ❖❖
WORKING IN BOTSWANA

By this time, we already had three children, a girl and two boys. We agreed with my wife that I would be the only person who will reside in Botswana while the rest of the family continued to stay in Zimbabwe. It would not have been practicable to relocate with my wife since she was in a teacher training college. The three children were attending school. Leaving my family behind dampened my spirits.

My journey to Gaborone, Botswana was overnight but I was comfortable since I had booked a sleeper. By 8am, I had reached the place.

I went straight to the ministry of health offices who deployed me to Sekgoma Memorial Hospital in Serowe. In the afternoon, I boarded a train to my new station and since I arrived late in Palapye, I put up there.

The next day, the driver from Sekgoma picked me up very early in the morning. As the place was not very far, we took about forty-five minutes.

On arrival at my station, the driver took me to the

administrative block. After welcoming me, they nominated a nurse who showed me round the hospital. I liked all the departments because they were well equipped and the staffing levels for doctors, nurses and all auxiliary workers were quite good.

They supplied me with uniforms and after that; they drove me to the hotel where I was booked in for two weeks. That was real red carpet treatment.

The following day, I reported for duty and they placed me in Maternity Department and I did not expect to have trouble because of the valuable experience I had gathered in my country. The only immediate problem I experienced was the language barrier, as most patients did not speak English, but Setswana. I was unable to speak a word in their local language.

I immediately devised a system to counter this language problem, as I understood the importance of knowing the patient's language in order to perform my nursing duties well. Without that barrier, the patients would feel free to express their problems.

I took a pocket notebook and wrote all the common phrases used like greetings and also made a translation of the language used in Maternity Department. I did that with the help of the local nurses. After mastering what I had written, I continued to expand on my vocabulary, and gradually it became richer. The progress I made within that short period seemed to impress my workmates.

I also met a Dutch doctor who had been in the country a few years before me and his fluency in Setswana motivated me. I asked him to give me the recipe and he was very keen to assist. He had learnt the local language by using audio cassettes that came with a book and he was ready to sell to me if interested. I could not turn the offer down since it came with a reduced price. The acquisitions from the doctor were of great help as it enhanced my chances of learning the language quickly.

Despite the language handicap, the patients did not resent me. I think the general influx of foreign workers in the country had influenced the community to become receptive. They had also realised I was trying hard to learn their language.

Working with the staff was not very difficult because quite a good number were foreigners. Since we came from different countries, our languages were different our medium of communication became English. Even most local nurses were open to communicate with us in English

After the expiry of my hotel stay, the hospital allocated me a private house. The house was quite big with three bedrooms, lounge, kitchen, spacious veranda, separate toilet and bathroom. It was also in a lovely area. My employers subsidised my rental and except for a few luxuries, they had fully furnished the house.

Out of the work place, I interacted with many people one of whom was Mr Rodgers Thombozi, a teacher from Malawi. We shared the same spiritual beliefs but he was more mature than I was. With time, we became close and he had a pivotal role in my spiritual growth.

After acquiring the local vocabulary, it became the norm to hear foreigners communicating amongst themselves in Setswana. I think this multicultural experiences was of immerse benefit to the country.

Working in Botswana proved very fruitful as my life improved tremendously and apart from the international experience I hoped for, my financial status shot up. That enhanced my family life style and my salary managed to cover our needs as well as helping my parents in the village. My wife had also completed teacher training and her salary boosted our income.

As the Botswana Government paid the primary schools fees for the children of the expatriate workers who remained in their native country, I managed to transfer my children to private schools. My youngest child enrolled at a prestigious pre-school at the age of three and within a short space of time, he was fluent in English. That was a giant step in contrast with me who started learning English at age of nine. I only gained fluency in English at my seventh year in primary school.

I managed to change furniture for my house in Zimbabwe as well as buying a few luxuries for my new residence in Botswana. Soon we owned luxury items like videocassette recorders which reminded me of one of my wedding organiser who scoffed at the idea of capturing my wedding day on a video tape.

Since then then, the education standard in Zimbabwe was better than in Botswana, my family remained in my country for our children's education and that did not affect our relationship because I visited home twice or thrice a month. My wife and children visited Botswana every school holiday. My children enjoyed the visits so much because in Botswana grocery, toys and clothes were cheaper. I bought my wife a car to help her with the upkeep of children.

I also managed to clear the mortgage for our family house, renovated and extended it. As a way of contributing to Nemane, the place of my birth, I bought land and built a general dealer shop and it became the largest in the community.

The comfort experienced by my children was so much that when I told them of my past they could hardly believe me. One day I drove them to the one-room accommodation I used to stay in with my sister, Sophie. Strangers now stayed in there since Sophie vacated the place years back when the council upgraded her accommodation. I wanted my children to see my roots and appreciate that good living comes after a struggle and my other reason was to encourage them to work hard in life. Even after we visited the place, they still could hardly believe me, especially my youngest son.

Working outside the country had completely transformed our life and at one time, we owned three vehicles. I remember one day after taking a walk with my wife, we were standing outside our house, and my wife said, "Did you ever think we could own so many cars?"

I did not reply, but instead, I just looked at her and smiled.

After five years of working in Sekgoma Memorial Hospital, they transferred me to Maun General Hospital with three other midwives. The hospital had a critical shortage of midwives so we were to fill that gap.

That was the same year my Dad died. He died at the age of eight-three from old age. By that time, my Mum was seventy-nine. My Mum and my Dad's third wife continued to stay in the homestead, his second wife had been dead two years ago and my Dad's two younger wives had already deserted him. Before my Dad died, they had moved to Samahuru Village which was more or less like Vulashaba, only that it was less sandy.

I did not like the transfer to Maun because I had been accustomed to Serowe. Maun was also a well-known place for soaring temperatures and the idea of blistering heat did not go well with me. Maun further doubled my distance to Zimbabwe and for that reason my wife was also unhappy about the transfer. Surprisingly, it was welcome to the children especially the youngest as they fancied the idea of exploring the new world.

At our new post, in Maun, they put all the midwives in Maternity Department with the exception of me who they allocated to the Accident and Emergency/Outpatients Department. At first, I did not like the idea, since I had a great interest in midwifery. However, I adjusted within a short period, since I had worked in that department before.

One of duties in there was to escort patients flown to bigger hospitals for further management, a duty which needed high responsibility and expertise as some of those patients were critically ill or badly injured. In most cases, the nurse flew just with the pilot and in very rare cases; they would add an auxiliary nurse. It was a challenge I accepted with sheer determination. It was also the first time I flew.

When still going to the destination, I did not see much of the outside as my prime duty was to care for the patient, making sure the patient remains in a stable condition until the other hospital took over.

After handing over the patient to the referral hospital, we flew back. My first experience flying was exhilarating and it was wonderful to gain aerial views. I enjoyed the plane soaring into the clouds.

Sometimes the pilot usually asked me to sit next to him in the cockpit on the co-pilot's seat. He would then explain how the plane operated. Wow, I liked that experience!

Maun is a malaria-prone place and plans were in place to monitor that menace. The hospital ran yearly studies of the efficacy of sulfadoxine-pyrimethamine, a drug commonly used to treat malaria. It selected me to be in charge of that programme giving me an opportunity to be in involved in many malaria seminars.

I attended some seminars as a participant and others as a facilitator and I acquired massive experience in the prevention and treatment of malaria during those seminars. I also had the privilege of flying in bigger planes to attend national conferences. My exposure to research gave me the other side of nursing which was challenging and exciting.

I soon discovered the beauty of Maun, a tourist resort area and the gateway to the famous Okavango Delta. The place was always a hive of tourism with visitors coming in and out and was also not short of entertainment as it boasted several hotels and lodges. If one felt bored, a walk-in game park was within easy reach. The park was home to less dangerous animals like zebras, kudus, wildebeests, giraffes and baboons. It was a pleasure to watch the animals at close range.

The shopping mall was much bigger than the one in Serowe. Maun had almost all essential shops like the ones found in capital city, Gaborone. Sometimes I would visit the mall for either shopping or simply for a walk.

The only problem with Maun was its unpredictable and unfavourable weather. In summer, day temperatures averaged about 36 degrees Celsius (95 Fahrenheit). Sometimes the temperatures hit 40 degrees (105 Fahrenheit). To be comfortable in our houses, we used air-conditioning.

One year after my Dad's death, we decided that my Mum should leave the village and stay with my wife in Bulawayo. Before that, I used to tell her it was high time she joined us and she would say she preferred rural life. One day, I drove to collect her from the village, although she was adamant, but with more persuasion, she agreed.

It took her some months to adjust to the city life and when she had adapted she loved the place. When we go to our church, she would sometimes accompany us and one day she decided she wanted to be a Christian. We made arrangements and she was baptised and not long after Sophie followed suit.

The foreign workers of Maun General Hospital workers decided to form an association. That association was a brainchild of Oriedi, a foreign nurse from Kenya. She brought the idea to me and I accepted it. We then informed all the foreign workers in the hospital and they accepted it. The membership included doctors, nurses, radiographers and laboratory staff.

We called that association Afya, a word meaning health in Swahili. We realised that we came far from home and in times of trouble, we had no one to lean on. It could be in times of illness, accidents or even death.

We contributed monthly to the association fund and when a member left Maun on transfer or otherwise, a farewell party and a gift was organised for him. At the end of the year, we organised Christmas parties, our spouses and children were welcome to join us. The association was able to knit the expatriates together.

I worked for five years in Maun and in total; I worked for ten years in Botswana. I will always cherish my stay in that country because everyone was welcoming and I gained immense knowledge. I became fluent in the local language and that made me part of the community.

My curiosity to gain international exposure was inclined to working in a developed country. I therefore arranged to relocate to the United Kingdom by registering my nursing qualifications with the Nursing and Midwifery Council for that country. The process was very long as among other things, it involved sending my training transcripts.

❖31❖
IN GLASGOW {42 years old}

Six months after, the council registered my qualifications and I was thrilled to bits as it meant that I could seek employment in that country. The agency I engaged, secured me a job in a nursing home in Hamilton, Scotland. I had no experience working in a nursing home as all my experience was in a hospital setting. Nonetheless, I accepted the offer and looked forward to the challenges.

After saving my notice of resignation in Botswana, I finally returned to my country, Zimbabwe, to bid my family farewell. We decided that I travel first and settle before the rest of the family joined me. My wife had to remain for a while supervising the final touches of our dream house which was under construction in the posh Burnside suburb.

I approached my mother about the new development, but this was not good news to her. She only felt better when I reassured her that although she would remain under Sophie's care, I would continue to support her.

The last few days, I made sure everything was in order, as I did not want to overstretch my wife when I have left.

The morning before I departed, I was busy receiving friends, relatives and neighbours who had come to bid me farewell. We joked and laughed as we prepared for that long separation.

As the time to leave drew near, we prepared ourselves to go to Bulawayo airport. Many people were willing to see me off to Glasgow, but transport let most of them down since we only had three cars. The lucky ones packed themselves in those cars and we drove to the airport. With no much time left, I quickly checked in, hugged my family and friends and then rushed to board the plane.

My dream journey to Glasgow had started. My heart was full of joy as I thought of my final destination. I flew to Johannesburg, South Africa by Air Zimbabwe. From there, I would catch my connecting flight. Flying did not excite me as I had done that several times when I worked in Botswana. However, I was ecstatic because I was to use KLM airways, one of the biggest airliners. I had only seen adverts about the airline some ten years back which portrayed a giant swan taking off from the sea and I found that spectacular. I always imagined their planes were massive and comfortable and my wish was to fly in one of them some day. The agency had made the travelling arrangements and by coincidence, they booked me with that airline. My dream had come true indeed.

An hour later, Air Zimbabwe touched down at Johannesburg Airport. On arrival, I walked around the airport terminals. Johannesburg airport is highly developed and I could not make head or tail of where I was and was thankful for the instructions that were on electronic boards. I had four hours connection time and I spent that time window-shopping. Since the airport is big, I had lots to see. They sold many beautiful items, which included clothing, jewellery and electronic goods.

When the time to depart drew close, I proceeded to board KLM and was not disappointed. The plane was undoubtedly gigantic and seating hundreds of passengers. I located my seat, which was next to a window.

Although my journey was an eleven hours flight, it was enjoyable and comfortable. The cheerful crew members kept us well fed throughout the flight. The video films screened kept me occupied.

By early morning hours, the plane landed at Amsterdam airport I was yet to catch another connecting flight to Glasgow. I was extremely impressed by the Amsterdam airport. It was massive, even bigger than the Johannesburg one. Everything about that airport was wonderful, classic and technologically advanced.

I had two hours waiting time before my connection to Glasgow, and during that time, I moved around the duty-free shops. When the time came, I then headed to Scotland. After an hour and a half's flight, the village boy landed in Glasgow.

I was so delighted to reach my destination. I found Glasgow to be a city of scenic views with splendid ultra-modern high-rise buildings combined with historical buildings. The fine motorways with its interlocking bridges drew my utmost attention. Everything was eye-catching, showing advanced technology and development.

I worked in the nursing home for three months and I enjoyed most interacting with the old folk. After that, I decided to leave the nursing home for a hospital setting because I could not fully apply my hospital nursing skills.

I secured a job at the Southern General Hospital, in Glasgow. It was in an Accident and Emergency Department, a very big place. It is well equipped with advanced equipment, but I braced myself for that great challenge and looked forward to my new job.

My two sons joined me after two months. With the help of my new British friend, John Wilby, I had made all the necessary plans for their schooling. They adapted well into their new environment.

Four months after the arrival of the boys, my wife joined us. This was after rounding off our projects. My daughter is still in Zimbabwe because she is married there.

I may not have achieved what other people might call highest esteem. Yes, I am not a celebrity or a prominent politician, but I am very grateful for what I have achieved. I thank God for giving me determination and a good framework of mind when things seemed impossible and the future looked very bleak.

Every time I reminiscent of my past life style and compare it to my present status, I do not feel proud. It humbles me and gives me hope and courage to face the hurdles that might stand on my way.

ABOUT THE AUTHOR

Calvin Ndlovu was born in 1960 in Nemane Village. Nemane is a remote village located in Tsholotsho District, Zimbabwe. Calvin comes from a very big and complex family. His father was a polygamist and had many children. Calvin is the last born child from his father's first wife.

He is a qualified registered nurse and midwife. He has worked for the Ministries of Health in Zimbabwe and Botswana. Currently, he works as a staff nurse in one of the hospitals in Glasgow.

He is married to Sikhangezile and together they have three children, a daughter and two sons. Apart from the girl, Calvin and the rest of the family now live in Scotland, United Kingdom. Calvin is a member of the Seventh Day Adventist Church.

Printed in Great Britain
by Amazon

65921183R00099